CALLWEY

TIM RAUE
MY WAY

TIM RAUE
MY WAY

CALLWEY

BAHNHOF ZOO
Täglich 20.00 Uhr
Tickethotline
0700 - 66 66 66 11

park inn

KFC
AUERMUSEUM THE
HAUS AM C
YOU ARE ENTERIN HE AMERICAN SECTOR
CARRYING WEAPO OFF DUTY FORBIDDEN
OBEY FFIC RULES
ВЫ ВЕЗЖАЕТЕ МЕРИКАНСКИЙ СЕКТОР
НОСИТЬ ОРУЖИЕ ЗАП ЕНО В НЕСЛУЖЕБНОЕ ВРЕМЯ
ПОВИНУИТЕСЬ РОЖНЫМ ПРАВИЛАМ
VOUS ENTREZ DA LE SECTEUR AMÉRICAIN
DEFENSE DE PORTER D RMES EN DEHORS DU SERVICE
OBÉISSEZ AUX
SIE BETRETEN D
CALZEDONIA
HOTEL
Wall

HARPER
S ARMY
OKPOINT
30
ZONE
TAXI
TAXI
TAXI

Zu breit

aerztezentrum 147
ROSSMANN
DB
WILLKOMMEN BEI McDONALD'S
Märkische Kiste
1961
Berlin Friedrichstraße

OF FRIEDRICHSTRASSE
GERRY WEBER
U
Friedrichstraße
NH COLLECTION
STARBUCKS COFFEE

park inn

Café Alibi

MÖBEL - OLFE

PART 03

recipes

K

I've been here before
But always hit the floor
I've spent a lifetime running
And I always get away
But with you I'm feeling something
That makes me want to stay

SAM SMITH
WRITING'S ON THE WALL

This book tells my story, my way from the gutter in Kreuzberg to the culinary starry skies. It is the way of a little guy from Berlin, who thanks to Prussian diligence, strength of will, ambition, discipline. and structure braved the storms and abysses of life to become one of the best chefs in the world.
It was, and still is, a long way, and I was lucky never to have to walk it all alone. My present business partner and former wife of many years, outstanding co-workers, and my best friends were always there by my side. Without them, none of this would have been possible.

The book begins with my biography, focusing on the links between Berlin and Singapore, because it was there, after visiting the *Jade* Restaurant in 2004, that my approach to cooking changed dramatically. For me, Singapore was the culinary turning point in my life, and it remains the city that massively inspires me today.

Berlin is my hometown; it has been buzzing and vibrating since the fall of the Wall in 1989. Berlin is full of life and continuous changes which have also influenced my life; it is the city where I grew up as a boy in the gutter, and where today I run several restaurants. Most of the recipes in this book originated in the kitchen of *Restaurant Tim Raue*, but it also contains a few recipes from my other restaurants, which are perfect examples of the way we cook there.

Join me for a while on my journey. Take a look at my world, at my totally egocentric, completely subjective, and utterly unmodified universe.

TIM RAUE

In this book, Tim Raue, one of Germany's top chefs, shares his personal and culinary life story. He tells his story in a remarkably open, hard, and direct way, while simultaneously being contemplative and permitting much deeper insights.

Tim Raue polarizes opinion: You like him or you don't. He doesn't make it easy for himself, and even less so for others. If you label him "egocentric" he can live with that. But a Tasmanian devil? That was yesterday.

His path to becoming a chef with two *Michelin* stars and being ranked number thirty-four in the list of the *World's 50 Best Restaurants* has been long and arduous. Without discipline, persistence, and willpower this special honor and worldwide acclaim wouldn't have been possible.

When Tim Raue tells us about his not-at-all-easy childhood, he's not asking for pity. He explains his progress, which he achieved all alone. His way could easily have led to another — dubious — career, but he says, "I never wanted to land back in the gutter". Thank God he applied his abundant energy to the kitchens of Berlin. We gourmets are grateful for that.

To be exceptional and to create exceptional dishes — this was his aspiration. In addition to boasting creativity and professionalism, he was also fortunate. Fortunate to be able to work toward success with his present business partner, Marie. He refers to *Restaurant Tim Raue* as "our lifetime achievement". Fortunate that his chefs and his team loyally stand by his side. In the process he has learned that a strong chef also needs a strong team.

Those who discover Tim Raue's cuisine will be overwhelmed by the flavors that transform his dishes into exceptional, long-lasting taste sensations. Asian influences characterize his cooking, but from his other projects we can see that he may also turn his attention to traditional Berlin dishes.

With his culinary art and his spirit of enterprise, Tim Raue has powerfully enriched Berlin as a gourmet location. The dining public has become truly international. Offering the very best in gastronomy remains a daily struggle. Tim Raue is a fighter. He resolutely continues along his way.

We look forward to seeing what surprises Tim Raue will dish up for us in the future.

KLAUS WOWEREIT
MAYOR OF BERLIN, 2001–2014

PART 01

finding yourself

PART 01

finding yourself

RAGE AND VIOLENCE

CHAPTER 01

I hear the shouts of encouragement from my boys, but I can't see them. My field of vision has narrowed to a small twenty-inch by twenty-inch square. Adrenalin is rushing through my body, and the glaring sun overhead is blinding me. Meanwhile, the U-Bahn (subway) screeches its way along the elevated track, into Kottbusser Tor station.

1991
With my classmates,
Hector Peterson High School

I feel like Jean-Claude van Damme in *Bloodsport*. As if I were in a kickboxing ring in Thailand — screams, adrenalin, thousands of eyes on me, the moment of truth. *Just go in for the blow*, I hear Paco's words in my ear, *don't waste time with idle chitchat*. The boy he was talking about suddenly appears in my square tunnel of focus. He's a person of color who has spoken ill of me. He's flanked by his crew from the mixed block of flats next to Kottbusser Tor; Yugoslavs, Germans, Africans. Behind me is my gang, the *36 Boys*; Turks, Arabs, Paco the Greek, and me, Tim, the only German.

"You never kick anyone who's on the floor; that's our code."

It's my first one-on-one fight: No knives, no baseball bats; just fists and the feeling of being on a street with a truck hurtling towards you. You can't get around it, you can't turn back, you can't do anything about it. The only way is to go through it. *Right in the kisser*, Paco's words still echo in my head, *you need to land the first punch*.

The boy is growing larger and larger in my square field of vision, every muscle and fiber in my body is tense, I see him open his mouth to say something, but he doesn't get that far. My fist hits him in the face, and he topples backward. A head full of screams, shouts, and buzzing. I immediately jump forward and kick him in the stomach. He manages to pick himself up, but his resistance is futile. I pound him in the face and stomach region, and then he's done. Completely out of breath and raging like a bull, I let go of him, my crew pulling me back. You never kick anyone who's on the floor; that's our code.

My reputation has been defended, and honor has been restored. I feel a friendly pat on the back, and hear some muttering. My field of vision gradually broadens again, I'm getting my bearings back. We're standing on Oranienstrasse, and someone sticks a fag in my mouth..

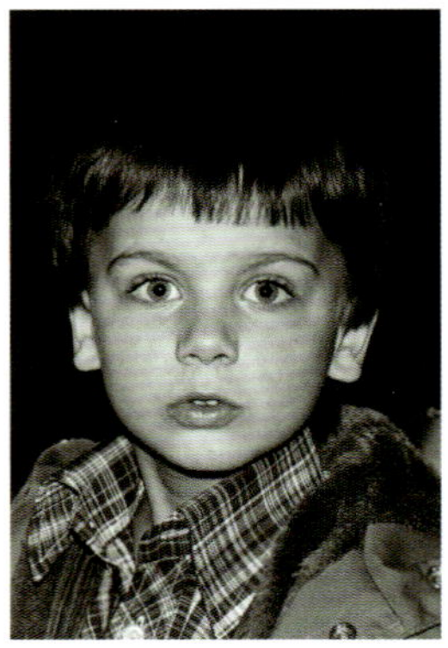

1981
Young and curious

A lot has already been said and written about my time with the *36 Boys*, about my time as a member of a youth gang which formed in Berlin-Kreuzberg in the late 1980s, and whose name was based on the district's former postcode, SO 36 (south-east 36). The gang was a bunch of petty criminals — or, at least, would-be petty criminals.

I have never tried to deny this phase of my life, or the violence it involved. These were formative years for me; they taught me toughness, they allowed me to feel part of a family at a time when no one else cared about me. At the same time, they were a reaction to my dark childhood days, and it is very important for me to explain how I ended up there: I wasn't part of a gang because I wanted to be out of control causing mischief or because I was born a sadistic thug. I was actually a lovely little boy until the age of about nine.

I was charming, kind, and considerate. I lived with my mother in a humble abode in the Berlin district of Kreuzberg, was outgoing, and had lots of friends. In other words, I was a completely normal child. My life revolved around going to school; I had good grades and had no behavioral problems. Our home was a bit shabby, and instant packet soups were the staples of my diet. But the occasional visits to Middle Eastern snack bars or pizzerias, when my mother could afford it, were an early culinary highlight. The soft, warm breads served at the Middle Eastern restaurants were a particular hit with me. I loved dunking them into the warm sauce.

When I turned nine, however, my life changed drastically. I was an only child, and my mother was unable to cope with raising and feeding an inquisitive young boy. So my parents, who separated when I was three, decided I would move to live with my father, who had since started a second family in Baden-Württemberg. This marked the start of a violent spiral, the effects of which continue to shape my life today. I may not have become a *Michelin*-starred chef had it not been for the destructive force instilled in me during that time, and which I still battle against every day, thirty years on. And this doesn't mean I take a less harsh view of, or even forgive the physical violence my father unleashed on me. From age nine to thirteen, which I spent living with him in Weil der Stadt and then — after a brief interlude back in Berlin with my mother — in Bruchköbel, in the state of Hesse, I was punished for the smallest offences. I was flogged if I messed up at school, and often had the living daylights whacked out of me if my bike got a scratch on it.

It was only logical that my earliest instincts included looking for the quickest shortcut and cleverest excuse to stay away from home. And so it was that, once in Bruchköbel (the second town I had to follow my father to), I got involved with Eintracht Frankfurt soccer hooligans through a slightly older boy named Jörg. I sat in their pubs, sang Böhse Onkelz (Evil Uncles) songs with them, went through the highs and lows on the soccer field, and got an initial taste of the feeling which grew stronger with the *36 Boys* after my return to Berlin: That of being part of a community, having a sense of security, and being bulletproof in this little kingdom. Later, with the *36 Boys*, it was never about where you came from, what your story was, or what your school grades were. It was about sticking together, about knowing that, whenever any problem arose, you would always have five people behind you, even if you were facing twenty opponents.

I now believe in the saying *Life is not about finding yourself — it is about creating yourself*. But it's a view which does take a while to accept. As a child who suffered domestic violence, I wanted to find something very specific: approval, a foothold. And I got this from soccer hooligans, for whom my role was eventually to ensnare groups of rival fans. I would run up the street yelling provocative slogans, and then shoot off if they started pursuing me. I was also quite a nimble little fellow, who had a bit of talent and a solid left foot on the soccer field, but who lacked any strong soccer-playing ambitions. While I did stir up some of my teammates, just as I did later on during the first few years in the kitchen with my chefs, it was for the same reason which shaped all my cooking stints: I hated losing. It annoyed me and affected me at a very deep level I didn't yet understand.

The hooligans, however, didn't just get into clashes with other groups of fans; they also fought with punks and anyone else who came along. They even sorted out some kids who kept laying into me at school. When I was 13, Stefan taught me self-defense. Stefan had a mighty British bulldog tattooed on his arm, and showed me how to protect my head with the right cover, or how to strike out from a position of self-defense. We simulated attacks and defense, split-second advances and counterattacks out in the fields, sometimes even in groups of four or six.

This training was soon also reflected in my behavior. I was now no longer the innocent child who had left Berlin. I was going through puberty, on the way to being a teenager; I had grown and become broader. I had two solid legs, whose specialty was the low-kick, a full-tilt kick to the thighs, which left few people standing afterwards. I occasionally drank alcohol to demonstrate my membership, and I only entered my father's house with the greatest reluctance. One evening, after I had returned home from a day out with Jörg, my

"But the occasional visits to Middle Eastern snack bars or pizzerias (...) were an early culinary highlight."

1981
With Grandma Gerda on the balcony of her apartment in Berlin Charlottenburg. I'm not yet interested in kitchen work

1981
Reluctantly having my hair done

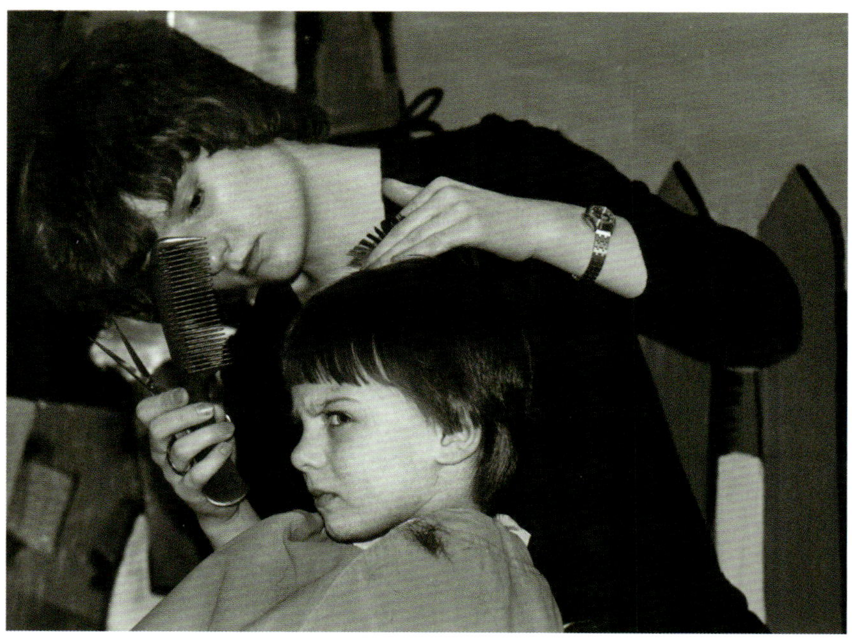

father was waiting for me in the living room. He barked at me, asking where I had been, saying that I had drunk alcohol, and that I was a stupid good-for-nothing, who would never achieve anything. He shoved me and was about to strike out, but I dodged it and threw him to the ground. Something in my look told him to stay down. It was to be the last time that he would try to beat me. I've had this look in me ever since. It continues to be an expression of the nuclear power plant of evil which this childhood humiliation sowed in me. For a long time, it would serve as my weapon, as a non-verbal fist which nipped any discussion in the bud. Only with time have I managed to bring it under control, and used this energy to create sensuous dishes.

I finally returned to Berlin just before my fifteenth birthday. Full of anger, and an instinct which has accompanied me ever since: to destroy anything that endangers me. Politically, I was neither right nor left wing, but, if nothing else, I could certainly identify with the Kreuzberg catchphrase coined by the rock band Ton Steine Scherben: *Mach kaputt, was dich kaputt macht (destroy whatever destroys you)*.
The nine-year-old boy who had left the city six years prior had become a ticking time bomb of dormant rage and aggression in search of an outlet. Anger not only manifested itself in me through swearing and cursing, but would also inevitably culminate in the need to grab the nearest chair and bash the other person over the head with it.

I was back living with my mother in Kreuzberg, near Schlesisches Tor, when I noticed

1985
Playing soccer with my cousins in the grounds of the Federal Garden Show (now the Britzer Garden) in Berlin Britz

"The nine-year-old boy who had left the city six years prior had become a ticking time bomb of dormant rage and aggression in search of an outlet."

2016
The banks of the Spree River in Berlin Kreuzberg

a couple of figures wearing the same bomber jackets, bearing the words *36 Boys*. They were my age, and I quickly recognized the parallels with my life: They spent most of their time out of the house, on the street. We were all about graffiti, hip-hop, and American street culture in general. And the fact that we were living in West Berlin, which was cut off from the rest of West Germany by the Wall, and which was labeled a ghetto after the Wall had fallen, made things easier. But the *36 Boys* didn't just roam the streets; they ruled them. Like me, their members came from socially disadvantaged backgrounds, and were mostly of Turkish, Arab, or Kurdish origin. There were no Germans in the gang, but I remained insistent. I wanted to be part of it, and was allowed to go through the initiation ritual soon after: a fight against two of the *36 Boys*. The aim of the fight wasn't just to show you were a tough cookie; it was also to prove you wouldn't run away in crucial situations, that you would instead stand side by side. After all, the streets weren't ruled with funny slogans; they were ruled with respect.

Gang life was, of course, not on an American scale. We were in Germany, not Los Angeles. We weren't players in a drug war killing people, but you can still cause a lot of harm to someone using knuckle-dusters, baseball bats, and knives. There were some minor drug offenses, and we would mug people too: the main object of desire was sneakers. You could also become a member, or at least be protected by the *36 Boys*, if you had artistic talent. My talent, however, wasn't rapping, break-dancing, or graffiti; it was my ability to run on ahead. I would walk right up to an opponent, I was a revolver which sat loosely in its holster, whose bullets usually hit their target. This would always come in handy, especially in a city which not only had the *36 Boys*, but also other youth gangs in other districts, like the Giants in Charlottenburg. No one knew exactly how many *36 Boys* there were; it wasn't a tightly regulated network, and no one kept a members' file. The core group consisted of about 20 people, and I soon became one of them. In most cases, we never knew each other's last name, exact ethnic background, or our parents' political preferences. We weren't interested in any of that. We were about forming a group to combat the adults' lack of understanding, and create a feeling of pride. That's what united us.

My parents, guardians, therapists, and teachers always underestimated my intellect. I would tell some what they wanted to hear, and wouldn't listen to the others. Right from being a child in Bruchköbel, I had not only undertaken martial arts training with the hooligans, but also retreated to my own private places. I had found an old caravan, which was only used on weekends, at a camping ground, and used this as a dwelling. I had broken into it and not told anyone. In the safety of my hideout, I had read magazines like *Spiegel* and *Stern*, and, after my initial experiences with the aromatic breads at the Middle Eastern restaurants in Berlin, culinary delights had returned to my life. I had eaten self-made salad and bread rolls, leafed through books, learned English, and imagined myself in another world, where I could step out of the caravan and not have to think: Who are we going to punch in the face today?

I still need these time-outs even today: moments when no one is around me, when I have no commitments or obligations, when it's just time for myself. That's when I'm able to invent things, create ideas about new dishes, or improve existing ones.

I still have these two sides: one being that of the Tasmanian Devil, the maniac who doesn't just break barriers, but pulverizes them; the driving force of his crew, who, even with sarcoidosis, ties himself to the stove so he doesn't fall over. And the other being that of sensitivity, subtlety, and muses in my cooking. These are the two poles between which my life plays out. During my early days as a chef in particular, the pendulum was swinging clearly toward the side of insanity.

Workdays began at five o'clock in the morning and finished at one o'clock the following morning, for months on end, with no day off, and no regard for others — or myself. Today, I have a slightly different definition of balance. Today, I slip into my blue chef's jacket and I'm Tim Raue, the chef. And when I take the jacket off, I'm Tim, the person. While this Tim is of course still constantly busy with cooking and his creations, it's not in that excessive, relentless manner. I ended up living excessively between the ages of 14 and 40, in a state of permanent output, of giving and providing, always using my own reserves. Now, however, I have created my own kingdom where things work for me. I blank out anything that's not important, and concentrate on what I'm all about: being exceptional, creating exceptional dishes, and delighting my guests. After a loved one called me egocentric, I looked up exactly what this meant. It denotes a person who creates their own circumstances and lives in them — and nothing could describe me better.

During my time with the *36 Boys*, it was my bomber jacket, not my chef's jacket, which defined me. But I wasn't just responsible for the physical stuff within the group. My erudition and eloquence saw me become the spokesperson for the *36 Boys*, and be their face, so to speak. One day, when the *Tageszeitung* daily newspaper was doing a feature story on Berlin's youth gangs, I met up with an editor at a café in Kreuzberg. He later referred to me as

1994
A brief period with blond hair. You learn from your mistakes

Rocky in his article, which I found insulting, and left me flushed with anger for weeks. But my intellect and ability to reflect on things did not show in my school grades. For my whole life, school to me meant stress, anger, frustration, and manipulation. Coupled with this were the many difficulties I faced due to constantly moving schools, as I was sometimes living with my mother in Berlin, and other times with my father in various cities. No one deemed it worthwhile to examine my talents more closely and say: Look at that, Tim has good social skills, is a fast problem-solver, and can motivate people. All they saw was the difficult student, the rebel, who herds his classmates around like a shepherd would his sheep; a rebel loudmouth destined to fall flat on his face in real life.

And to be honest, that was indeed the path destined for me. The path I forged was not. What saved me was my will, and the understanding that I had to look after myself, because I knew no one else would. I had ambition and willpower. I never dreamt the world would ever know about Tim Raue, nor did I imagine I would see my name on front covers. Never again did I want to end up in the gutter — and that was what spurred me on.

1998
Head chef at Kaiserstuben Restaurant, Berlin

PART 01
finding yourself

STRUCTURE AND DISCIPLINE

CHAPTER 02

Achieving the superhuman; always pushing and going beyond boundaries; keeping going when others fall; ignoring all the secondary things in life and focusing on your main work in progress, which also means yourself; following your own path despite all criticism, and creating something great out of it; knowing when to put your foot on the gas and when to sit back and leave things to others — these are the dogmas on which my success is based. But it all started with another factor: luck.

2016
Kottbusser Tor. Seemingly peaceful, this is one of the most dangerous squares in Berlin

"If I firmly believe in something, I jump right in."

______ Following the end of my school days, which culminated in me throwing my report card at the teacher's head and swearing never to return to a classroom again, I was quickly brought back to reality. It was called the BIZ, Berufsinformationszentrum (vocational information center), in Berlin-Kreuzberg, and it was soon after the fall of the Berlin Wall. There, a staff member devoid of any emotion took a pitying glance at my report cards and multiple-choice test and advised me that I would be suitable for three types of career: a gardener, a painter, or a chef. I rejected the first two immediately, but a chef sounded plausible. After all, the salads and bread rolls I had made myself in my secret caravan had brightened up those sad days in Bruchköbel. At that desk at the BIZ, I made my decision in the same way I have continued to make decisions throughout my life: without worrying about the consequences. No matter whether it's about assessing conditions at a cooking event which are different to those advertised by the organizer, taking the next step with my own restaurant, or opening a new restaurant, I don't stand there scratching my head thinking: *OK, now let's think about what we're doing.* I just keep driving. I briefly reduce the speed, because I can see three exits, but then quickly choose one and get straight back on the gas pedal. If I firmly believe in something, I jump right in. That's when I feel an enormous sense of optimism, almost euphoria, and am not concerned about what will happen if things don't work out. Failure is not an option. I simply operate on the assumption that I will invest as much energy and input as it takes so that they do work out. I look at it as if it were a matter of survival. And I established early on that I wanted to survive.

After my appointment at the BIZ, however, the accelerator initially only led me to dead ends. No restaurant or hotel kitchen was interested in a *36 Boy* from Kreuzberg who had only completed middle school, and who was described as "angry" in his conduct grades. The HR manager of the HOTEL PALACE at least went to the effort of telling me personally, face-to-face, that my report card marked me out as a troublemaker. Only then did I understand the gravity of my situation. I wanted to earn my own money, I wanted to stand on my own two feet, but, for the first time in my life, I realized I was being judged on what I had *not* done. All my applications were unsuccessful. I was still living with my mother, which was becoming increasingly unbearable. But one of the few teachers I hadn't ticked off during my school days put me in touch with a restaurant in the Grunewald, the CHALET SUISSE. She knew one of the managers there and put in a good word for me, and they were actually willing to give me a chance — one I nearly messed up on the very first day.

"I wanted to earn my own money, I wanted to stand on my own two feet, but, for the first time in my life, I realized I was being judged on what I had not done."

The problem with people from socially disadvantaged backgrounds is their total lack of discipline, which is apparent on multiple levels: You're not punctual, you don't finish things, you have no structure, you don't persevere. So it was that I arrived late for my trial day. I had completely underestimated the time it would take to get from Kreuzberg to the other side of the city. Fortunately, no one really seemed to notice, because the kitchen was already in chaos. I was placed at a station where I had to cut baguettes, and I can still picture the scene as if it were yesterday: A box of baguettes on the bench, which I had to cut into pieces for the bread baskets. I take a baguette out and start cutting, but after just the second baguette, I place two sticks on the board, then three, and look around for a longer knife. It may be a very simple example, but it shows that, right from day one, I was fast and efficient in the kitchen, and didn't ask whether I was allowed to do things that way or not. I proudly presented my pile of baguette pieces to the chef de partie, who looked at me as if I didn't know how to tie my shoelaces. Without saying a word, he pointed under the table, where there were another five boxes of baguettes, before flitting off again. Cursing and swearing, I did the rest of the baguettes — but I wasn't late again the next day.

I instead quickly realized the kitchen was my second home. I hurriedly found an apartment near my place of work, which soon distanced me from Kreuzberg and the *36 Boys*. But there were few places where my experiences as a street fighter could have been more useful than in my new job. On the

1994
Apprenticed for the third year at the Auerbach Restaurant, Berlin

one hand, the behavior and swear words used among the chefs were hardcore. Even the Frankfurt hooligans seemed like innocent lambs compared to the fierce, politically incorrect expressions uttered by chefs who were at the end of their tether. On the other hand, I was used to a completely different level of stress. They played two matches a day in the kitchen: one in the afternoon and one in the evening. But at CHALET SUISSE, a popular day-trip destination in one of Berlin's lushest areas, they also played mornings. This meant that nerves were always frayed, people would be shouting, swearing, and making threats, and everyone would be on a knife-edge at their station — yet, for the most part, it was like water off a duck's back for me. My idea of stress was a physical threat; my body would release adrenalin whenever I approached a pack of opponents. I did not consider a frenzied chef or the nervous blubbering of a headwaiter as reasons to lose my cool. My radar was used to going off for existential threats, not for things like how five chicken drumsticks were going to be ready to serve in the next two minutes.

This composure and inner peace were the foundations of my first days of training, along with Do you mean automatic reactions that quickly became second nature to me. Just as I had previously trained for physical battles in order to be able to act without thinking in crucial moments — thereby giving me a critical advantage — so I applied this philosophy to the kitchen. I cast everything else aside, and focused on memorizing automatisms to make my life easier: I would always put the knives and chopping boards in the same place, optimize every process, and repeat each action over and over again until it stuck. If someone were to wake me at three o'clock in the morning and ask for salt, I would know exactly where it was without having to think.

I was bad at dicing and cutting diamond shapes, so, after my fifteen-hour shift, I would spend hours practicing on carrots and celery roots while watching television. I trained for months, years. No one asked me to. I felt the need myself; I wanted to be able to do everything perfectly, without anyone having to specifically assign me to do it. This difference between duty and choice, between the applause on stage and the crap behind the scenes, is something I still need to keep demonstrating to the current generation of chefs: They need to distinguish between the illusion in the media and our real life at the stove. The illusion is that of high-flyers, awards and *Michelin* stars. But our daily business is a tough routine consisting of a constant balance between training and the actual game. That's why I like comparing the kitchen with the army; you have hierarchies and don't question everything.

These routine actions and the ability to optimize them gave me confidence in my training. I saw myself as a building with fixed pillars known as structure, accuracy, cleanliness, and precision — a view which in turn came from the two people who had always stood by me: my grandparents. Unlike their son — my father —, they had always looked after me as much as they could, even during the times I had lived with my mother. They had been the ones who put me in the bath when my hair once again hadn't been washed, and stuffed my clothes

"But our daily business is a tough routine consisting of a constant balance between training and the actual game."

1994
First position as head chef at Rosenbaum Restaurant, Berlin

into the washing machine. My grandmother cooked food using fresh ingredients, while my grandfather would accompany me to my football games. He worked as a representative for Bahlsen, the famous cookie maker, so there was always something sweet in the house, and later on I would also find the odd banknote in my trouser pocket. They lived in a small apartment in Berlin-Wilmersdorf, and were, of course, completely oblivious to the things I had done during my time as one of the *36 Boys* in Kreuzberg — partly also due to the fact that I would leave my bomber jacket at home when crossing Berlin, and thus the Giants' realm, to visit them. I never talked about it. I felt ashamed, because I knew they wouldn't understand the reason. As I grew older, however, it became clear to me that their lives worked well. Unlike every other adult who had influenced my life, they had their life under control, and that was largely thanks to the structure and discipline with which they organized their daily routine. Every object was in its place; the coffee cups sat six — not five or seven — centimeters away from the coffee machine. They left nothing to chance — and nor do I. The pieces in my sauce for Wasabi Langoustine, one of my signature dishes, are not two by three or four by two millimeters thick — they're exactly two by two millimeters. No more, no less.

It was this structure and precision which I also adopted during my kitchen training — and which ultimately also triggered my rapid rise. My palate may only have been at the start of its journey, but my ambition was already at world-champion level. I made sure that everything was neat and tidy, my station was clean when I arrived, and gleaming when I left. In the kitchen, it's all about winning; anything which distracts you from that must be gotten rid of. I give my chefs their freedom these days, but they can't have a Mickey Mouse mug at their station. One look at the cup, one second of lacking concentration, and a mistake is made. We can't afford that. The level we cook at only works with an absolute focus on that one essential element: the plate.

During those early days as a trainee, I didn't dream of being a *Michelin*-starred chef. I was just happy to have a job which ensured my survival and allowed me to have my own place to live. A daytrippers' haunt like the CHALET SUISSE is not somewhere you would think could ever mark the beginnings of a culinary journey — not when you start out as a patisserie trainee who commences work at 7 a.m. on any given summer's day, and churns out forty sheet cakes after beating 360 eggs in a giant bowl. And good luck with finding any piece of eggshell which falls into the mixture. But as I was a big fan of

1997
Rosenbaum Restaurant, with Anne-Marie Raue, third from the right, holding bottle

"I had found something I was good at, and I quickly also realized something else: I was able to operate at and sustain a pace most others couldn't manage."

efficiency even back then, I would throw all the eggs, including shells, into the bowl, run the whisk through them, then pass the entire mixture through a strainer. It was twice as quick and worked fantastically. An older patissier, however, who felt this was an insult to his professional honor, denounced my method to the head chef, forcing me to refrain from using it — at least when someone was looking over my shoulder. Of course I never accepted things like this lying down, and was always slapped with wonderful punishments for my big mouth. One of those meted out to the kitchen's most impertinent trainee was the task of trimming forty-four pounds of pigs' kidneys once a week. These were usually filled to bursting with urine, which made them cheaper to buy, and had to be rinsed in-house. It was basically an extravaganza of piss which would run down your arms. Disposable gloves weren't as common in kitchens as they are today. On this day, I took the S-Bahn (suburban railroad) home and sat opposite two girls, one of whom smiled at me. At least until the other one looked around the carriage, frowning, and said the smell was so bad some tramp must have pissed himself. I looked down, shoved my hands in my pockets, and got off at the next station.

But these inconveniences would not dim my growing desire and ambition. I had found something I was good at, and I quickly also realized something else: I was able to operate at and sustain a pace most others couldn't manage. Even during my first few days, I saw how the head chef was caught behind the eight ball when serving. I knew what the "Casimir" turkey curry with rice, baked bananas, and apple should look like, so I just started plating up and helping out — because I could see they still needed six more. This response was also the reason why I was able to keep the job despite being late on the first day. Just a few months later, I moved from the patisserie to the garde-manger, the cool pantry area where cold dishes are prepared. I bought magazines whose covers featured top chefs at the time like Siegfried Rockendorf, and my passion for cooking resulted in the realization that, beyond the daytrip world of the Grunewald, there were other, much

"(...) you didn't have to do things the way you had been taught as an apprentice, and you didn't have to comply with guests' expectations. You can also follow different paths. Indeed you must."

better restaurants where dishes weren't served with a ladle. While I had been lucky to even get the job at CHALET SUISSE, I now needed something more. I had gotten a taste of the chef's life, and had the Chamber of Commerce and Industry arrange for me to change workplaces in the middle of my apprenticeship.

So it was that I arrived at AUERBACH, a restaurant in Kreuzberg with a young, ambitious head chef, where I completed my training. It wasn't far from *36 Boys*' territory, but the switch to the chef's apron had also seen me hang up my bomber jacket. I was concentrating all my energy on my work, meaning my time at Kottbusser Tor quickly became a distant memory. I moved to SCHLOSS GLIENICKE soon after under the aegis of Johannes Klapdohr, one of the first key figures in my career. Although his fine creations had earned him fifteen *Gault Millau* points, and he had previously worked as a sous chef for Eckart Witzigmann, it wasn't so much his culinary skills in themselves which left their mark on me; it was his actions as a person and his outlook on life which impressed me. Klapdohr was only a few years older than me, which proved to me that chefs didn't have to be old, embittered gamblers who vented their frustration on younger generations. He was an eccentric who wrote to the German transport ministry to say he would consider any two-lane roads in Germany as 60 mph zones. Nor did he constantly have his head in cookbooks; he was also interested in scientific literature and gave lectures about the behavior of the bonobo monkey. What most impressed me, however, was the nonchalance with which he flouted the unwritten cooking laws which had been drummed into us during our training. Fish, for example, had to be scaled before handling; that was as incontrovertible as saying "amen" at the end of a prayer. You then had to gut it, fillet it, and bone it. There were five of us in the kitchen, and during the summer we would be sending out more than 200 covers, among them being the final products of our fisherman's entire zander (pike-perch) haul. It was absolutely impossible to prepare the zander using this laborious method. Klapdohr would quickly chop open the fish, cut out the fillet, pan-fry it with its scales, then simply wipe the crispy scales off — and serve it unboned. I of course found this quite a tough approach, but hierarchy is hierarchy. Klapdohr didn't ever shy away from experimenting with flavors either. One day, he asked me if I liked blood. I said no. He then promptly started baking blood in a pan in the oven, cut it into diamond shapes, garnished it with foie gras, glazed apple, and roasted onion, and presented it to me. It tasted incredible. He opened my eyes. I realized you didn't have to do things the way you had been taught as an apprentice, and you didn't have to comply with guests' expectations. You can also follow different paths. Indeed you must.

And that's exactly what I did.

PART 02

creating yourself

GAULT MILLAU
Deutschland
2005
Tim Raue
AUFSTEIGER
DES
JAHRES

PART 02

creating yourself

METHOD AND MADNESS

CHAPTER 03

After a few brief stints at places like the Bamberger Reiter, First Floor at the Hotel Palace, and Quadriga at the Brandenburger Hof, I started my first role as head chef at Kaiserstuben in Berlin-Mitte in 1998.

2004
With the *Gault Millau* guide's chief editor Manfred Kohnke and publisher Johannes Heyne at the Rising Star of the Year award ceremony

For the first time in my career, I bore sole responsibility for the culinary concept, and could design the menu exactly how I wanted it. As such, I reinterpreted traditional Berlin cuisine, which I had always had a weakness for, due in no small part to my grandmother's Falscher Hase (meatloaf stuffed with egg). I used high-quality ingredients, and gave my creations a flavorsome twist, like the Berliner Senfei (mustard eggs) with caviar, which was very popular among the guests.

2000
With Bernd Matthies (keynote speaker and journalist) and Volker Hassemer (my Berlin business partner) at the award ceremony for Berlin Master Chef of the Year

"All that counted was the perfect dish and happy guests."

The KAISERSTUBEN wasn't far from Museum Island and was well patronized, resulting in mentions in the specialist press, and increasing attention from the Berlin media, which reported on the talented, young, unconventional chef from Kreuzberg — a Berlin chef in Berlin was always worth a story. But my growing reputation would not save me from an unpleasant surprise. One day, our supplier was standing in the kitchen, heaving the utensils delivered by him back into his truck. He hadn't been paid for months, he told me angrily. Perplexed, I went to question my boss, but was myself soon also met with closed doors: The swindler had changed the locks. I had lost my job overnight, and would never receive my outstanding wages.

With this professionally emboldening, personally sobering experience behind me, I started my next job at the HOTEL RIEHMERS HOFGARTEN on Yorckstrasse in Kreuzberg, where I was not only head chef of the property's gourmet restaurant, E.T.A. HOFFMANN, but simultaneously also the hotel manager and staff chef. There may be people who would have been capable of holding this position in their mid-twenties, having prepared for it during their training. But I was a self-taught man who had boxed his way up from Kottbusser Tor — and who certainly had not relied on the fine art of diplomacy. During the job interview, I had followed the same motto I applied to everything: Just say you can do the required tasks, then learn them as you go and make them more efficient.

I soon left the operational side of the hotel to a staff member employed to handle such matters. I had come to take the E.T.A. HOFFMANN forward, and I now no longer considered the idea of earning a *Michelin* star a mere fantasy conjured up by a dreamer from the gutter. It was within reach; I could smell it. To achieve this, I wanted to further perfect my cooking, and optimize the path I had carved at the KAISERSTUBEN. I took my interpretation of Berlin cuisine (for which I had already made a name for myself), enhanced it with classic French cuisine or Mediterranean dishes, and garnished it with the odd Asian course. I cooked with high-quality products from all over the world, and offered my guests a culinary journey around the globe, which had its highlights, but also one disadvantage: It had no clearly defined line. Symptomatic of this phase was the pan-fried foie gras with three types of beans and caviar, which we churned out like no tomorrow.

We were a small team in the kitchen, and I was constantly cracking my whip at them. I was still that Tasmanian devil who made every decision, and who flipped if something went wrong.

One of my chefs — the only one who had followed me from the KAISERSTUBEN — loved reading books about gruesome mass murderers and psychopaths like Charles Manson at the time. One day, he told me in all seriousness that I would fit perfectly in the category of these types of people due to my social conditioning and character. That gave me pause for thought. I knew I was a bit crazy, but in a positive way. I didn't consider myself a sociopath or psychopath. But kitchens are microcosms of madness, and when the chaos became uncontrollable, that was when I snapped.

I had conditioned myself this way right from the very early days of my training: full focus and concentration on the moment, completely ignoring your own needs. All that counted was the perfect dish and happy guests. Even today, I can work eighteen hours without eating, drinking or satisfying basic human needs. When I let go and run the risk of becoming negligent, I always picture the two cyclists, Lance Armstrong and Jan Ullrich. Year after year they ride for the Tour de France title, meeting on the mountain to slug out the crucial stage. Both put in superhuman efforts and suffer unimaginable torture, but there's one difference: At the key moment, Jan Ullrich stays stuck to his seat, while Armstrong gets off it and refuels the tank with energy that's no longer even there. He creates distance and wins, and that's how I see myself too: When everyone else is tired, I get out of my seat and bring it home. I'm like Armstrong, except that I dope up on sugar. This immense willpower is one of my great strengths. But, as I later learned, not everyone has it.

"I grew not only as a chef, but as the captain of a team, who knew that a kitchen is only as strong as its weakest link."

So it was no wonder that no one from my kitchen followed me to the SWISSÔTEL Berlin in 2003, when I left the E.T.A. HOFFMANN and rejected the ownership share offered to me. At that time, my world revolved too much around me: *Who am I?, What am I?, What do I stand for?*. I was unable to delegate tasks and to allow other chefs to grow next to me. I never praised anyone, I only ever criticized — perhaps because I had never known anything different at home. But the five years spent at the luxury hotel on Kurfürstendamm would fundamentally change my thoughts and actions. I grew not only as a chef, but as the captain of a team, who knew that a kitchen is only as strong as its weakest link.

"I learned that you could also express your wishes with a smile, and that this method was actually very successful."

One of the people most responsible for this was the SWISSÔTEL director, Gerhard Struger, an Austrian who was hard to picture anywhere but on the bridge of his five-star ship. He largely gave me free rein with my culinary concept, but, from the very first day, would regularly take me aside and advise me to look at my situation from different perspectives: *Mr. Raue, everyone is happy with what you're doing in the kitchen,* he would say in his soothing and reassuring way, *but you're running a one-man show, and that doesn't work at a hotel.*

I had to relearn how to be part of a whole. At E.T.A. HOFFMANN, I didn't have to answer to anyone; at the SWISSÔTEL, I had to deal with various departments, which all contributed to the hotel's operations in their own way. Previously, I had been the one employing chefs; now, I had a human resources manager telling me in no uncertain terms: *No one's employed unless I sign!* These interactions were new for me, and I soon realized that, if I shouted instructions down the phone and banged it back down on the hook without waiting for the other person to respond, my jackets wouldn't come back from the laundry. The staff would rightly think, *screw him!*, and I would end up trudging to the laundry to iron the jackets myself.

Thus, some of my other traits became apparent. I brought out my eloquent side, which I had neglected in my bid to focus on getting ahead in the kitchen; which, like a plant in the shade of a mighty tree, was not getting enough light amidst all

2005
During a cookery course at the Swissôtel, Berlin

2006
With Grandma Gerda at the award ceremony for *Gault Millau* Chef of the Year

2007
In my role as Global Culinary Advisor at the Swissôtel Food & Beverage Conference, on the roof terrace of Swissôtel The Stamford, Singapore

the pressure I was under. It was the charm of the young boy who had secretly read magazines and comics in the shelter of his caravan in Bruchköbel and had dreamt of America, before the weight of reality had hauled him back out of his childhood fantasies. I learned that you could also express your wishes with a smile, and that this method was actually very successful. Only when it wasn't did the part of me that did not tolerate objections resurface.

I still acted like a hooligan in the kitchen, but I got better, due in no small part to the support of Gerhard Struger. While I continued to swear like a trucker and unleash a tirade of abuse on my chefs, I recognized that I had to take them along with me on the ride. I had to share my knowledge. I knew I would only be successful if I could inspire my staff and get them to develop under my leadership. I was nowhere near achieving an analytical cooperation like I have now at RESTAURANT TIM RAUE, but I was changing and creating something else: A loyal crew who, over those five years, screamed together, laughed together, bit each other's heads off, and comforted each other.

In short, I formed a gang as I had known it with the *36 Boys* right from a young age. My trick was to isolate our kitchen team from the rest of the enterprise. We simply didn't follow certain rules which applied to other departments. We knew it was us who set the pace, and there was no one who could threaten us. We called the shots, and the other departments knew it. I took the fall for my chefs, protected them when dealing with HR, and, when necessary, would take two crates of beer to the on-site engineers so we could get cable TV in the kitchen. Occasionally, a truckload of Häagen-Dazs without a delivery slip would go astray and find its way to us.

These things were important. I was still able to scare my staff with a single glance, but I was also the first to be up for a practical joke. I did know one thing: A kitchen didn't work without laughter and humor. Pressure, which reaches insane levels at our workplace, needs to be released, and if this can't happen there and then, it may do so at a bar after your shift or, worse still, at home. And we were certainly under pressure, because every day was like a fight for survival. At a five-star property like the SWISSÔTEL, there were banquets, room-service meals, breakfast buffets, and of course the 44, the gourmet restaurant I was leaving my mark on. All these different requirements had to be met at the various kitchen stations simultaneously; the burger and fries for room 234 had to be dished up at the same time as the six-course menu for the 44. The whole process was like a form of medieval torture, where each arm and leg was tied to a different horse with a rope. This constant grind not only required refined culinary virtuosos and delicate esthetes, but also animals who could plough through and deal with all the order slips.

Steam was let off in all kinds of ways. You could come into the kitchen and be hit in the butt with a paintball by one of the chefs. You had to be able to live with that, even as a chef. I would then hunt the person responsible down with a wooden spoon and everything would be fine again. We would wipe the paintball paint off the refrigerators, everyone had had their fun, steam had been let off, the valve was shut again, and we could refocus on our daily business. At each stage of your life, you get the chefs you deserve and who reflect you. At the SWISSÔTEL, we were a crazy bunch.

Our aim at the 44 was, of course, to earn our first *Michelin* star. Media attention had quickly grown following my arrival at Kurfürstendamm: In 2004, we had landed 17 *Gault Millau* points, and in 2005 I was named "rising star of the year." The latter particularly made me feel I had roots running twenty yards deep. I had a sense of certainty: I'm being noticed, I exist as Tim, the chef. The evolution I brought to the plate over these five years was just as immense. I became more precise and, for the first time, was using absolutely top-quality products.

From a flavor perspective, my time at the 44 was my most expressive; I was extremely generous with all the spices, and added a hefty dose of heat, sourness, and sweetness to my dishes — sometimes to the point of excess. One dish which typified this time was the Attersee ox with beet and black truffle. It was one of the first dishes where the presentation also demonstrated the path I was seeking to forge: clearer, more puristic, but still with impressive flavor. I did away with the global odyssey I had packed into the menu at E.T.A. HOFFMANN, instead dividing my cooking into Evolution and Revolution areas. The former represented the French-German cuisine we had based ourselves on, while Revolution stood for the further development we were striving for. However, what hardly anyone knew, was that, at this time, when I would finally achieve national recognition as a chef and have billboards of myself on buildings along the Kurfürstendamm, I was caught in a constant dichotomy. And I blame this on my first trip to Asia.

During the first few years of my training, and even during my days as a young head chef, my entire focus had been on cooking. I had subordinated my life to my ambition and my will to improve and get ahead. I didn't take vacations, or if I did, it would be to visit other haute-cuisine chefs of the time. I went to see Marco Pierre White in London, admired the magical creations of Juan Mari Arzak and Pedro Subijana in the Basque country, and was annoyed with Alain Ducasse in Paris over a table being placed next to the bathroom. I never saved anything my entire life; all my money went toward these trips. My accountant would shudder every time I boarded a flight. I saw these trips as a kind of continued education, and would soak it up like a sponge, be it the dishes, the furnishings, the porcelain, the glasses, the overall atmosphere, or the manner of the staff. Nothing bored me more than posing for a souvenir photo in front of the Eiffel Tower.

2004
With Mario Pattis, at the Davidoff Gourmet Festival, Berlin

But all these educational taster trips had always been limited to Europe or the United States. Until 2004, I had never been to Asia — and today sometimes I still wonder what would have happened if I'd gone earlier.

"I formed a gang as I had known it with the *36 Boys* right from a young age."

2006
Photo session to mark my being awarded my first *Michelin* star and *Gault Millau* Chef of the Year

"At each stage of your life, you get the chefs you deserve and who reflect you."

The SWISSÔTEL hotel chain was part of the Fairmont Raffles Hotels International group, which ran luxury hotels on every continent. My first Asia trip in 2004 took me to Bangkok and Singapore, home to the city-center SWISSÔTEL THE STAMFORD, which, soaring seventy-three floors up to a height of 741 feet, was the tallest hotel in Southeast Asia at the time. The trip was one big eye-opener; an explosion of flavors, a breathtaking combination of spice, zing, and palatability. It may have been my first time in Asia, but it felt as though I had come home. The standard of Chinese cuisine at Singapore's many Cantonese restaurants was completely new to me. It reached its climax at JADE with Sam Leong, a young head chef who added a contemporary twist to Chinese cuisine. He did away with the shared dishes that were part of Chinese dining traditions, and instead served the food in small, Western-style portions. At Jade, I sat like Genghis Khan in front of a sea of plates and cups because I couldn't stop ordering more. Everything tasted incredible. Especially the cod, which was sensationally crispy and served in a sweet-and-sour sauce with a Thai mango salad. It's a dish I today consider a turning point: Everything changed after that. The fish was of excellent quality and texture; it was crispy and soft at the same time. The dish also played with different temperatures, being warm and cold, and achieved a flavorsome fusion of sweetness, sourness, and intensity which nearly had me crying with pleasure. This combination of Thai and Chinese cuisine was an eye-opener. I ordered the dish a total of four times that first evening, and came back the next two nights as well. When the staff served me the fish with a knowing smile, I thought to myself: *Why do you still cook that French stuff? This is what you call fun; this is pure dining pleasure!*

It was with these thoughts in my mind that I flew back to Berlin. I was itching to incorporate what I had seen and tasted into my cooking. But it would be another three years before I actually dared to use these spices and flavors. My new ideas weren't feasible for a hotel like the SWISSÔTEL. I didn't want to serve rice, pasta, or potatoes, I didn't want lactose in any products, and I wanted to reduce the sugar content. This was not going to work for the types of guests staying at a big five-star hotel on Kurfürstendamm, with its many different requirements. But it's not like we dished up crap at 44 either.

"Never rest on your laurels, always aim to improve things — that was both his and my motto."

In 2007, I was named *Gault Millau* Chef of the Year, and then, when the annual lists came out in November, there it was: Tim Raue had earned his first star. It was a surreal moment; one which I had been working towards for years. It was the moment I had been putting above all else. When I heard we'd been awarded the star, however, I didn't shriek with joy or beat my chest like a gorilla. I enjoyed the whole thing the same way I had enjoyed all the special moments in my life: in silence, with a mixture of gratitude and humility. It may indeed be that I have difficulty experiencing joy. It makes me mistrustful, giving me the feeling that I haven't been careful enough, that I've dropped my guard. That's the one final remnant of the old street thug in me: Joy is the precursor to carelessness, and carelessness means problems. Nonetheless, the champagne corks were definitely popping in the kitchen after that news.

These awards in 2007 resulted in the name Tim Raue becoming more prominent, particularly the confines of Berlin. The SWISSÔTEL saw American tourists in Birkenstock sandals sitting right next to gourmets who had traveled across the whole country to dine with Tim Raue. I had reached a new level of fame, though my passion for Asia continued to blaze within me as brightly as ever. I thought to myself: *If I can earn a star for this vague, unstructured cuisine, what could I achieve if I did something I really loved? What would happen then?!*

I knew I would never be able to indulge this yearning at 44; I had reached the limit. Then Gerhard Struger left Berlin to relocate to the Istanbul hotel. Over the years, he had become a fatherly mentor to me, and I respected his advice. Just as I was obsessive about cooking, giving it priority above all else, he lived for the hotel, and strove to constantly improve. Never rest on your laurels, always aim to improve things — that was both his and my motto. His successor, however, did not share this enthusiasm. Suddenly, I was no longer dealing with a visionary, but rather an objector whose main focus was to ruffle no feathers and be liked by his staff. I felt I would not be able to develop further like this. I had changed, and my time at the SWISSÔTEL was drawing to an end.

Unlike at E.T.A. HOFFMANN, however, I knew this time that if I went, I wouldn't go alone. My battalion of chefs was ready to leave with me.

牛

2016
Chinatown, Singapore

PART 02

creating yourself

PRESENCE AND AUTHORITY

CHAPTER 04

The opening of Ma Tim Raue in Berlin in 2008 saw me really hone my cooking: I cooked Asian food from then on. The cornerstones of my dishes — sweetness, sourness, and spiciness — have remained the cornerstones of my dishes ever since. I became clearer and more precise, and nothing reflected this better than my interpretation of Peking duck, which I had spent years tweaking and refining. It is served on three plates, with a separate broth made from the duck's tongue, heart, and stomach.

"It was here that my ideals of Thai flavor, Japanese product perfection, and Cantonese-Chinese yum-yum food came to fruition."

2016
Evening meal at my favorite Cantonese restaurant in the Newton Hawker Centre, Singapore

______ My mission after moving from the SWISSÔTEL was simple: To quickly back up the star I had been awarded at 44 — and pocket the second star the following year. The UMA Restaurant located in the same complex was to be the country's best Japanese restaurant, and the GABRIELE the best Italian. I juggled these three balls as culinary director, but the finest of them all was MA TIM RAUE. It was here that my ideals of Thai flavor, Japanese product perfection, and Cantonese-Chinese yum-yum food came to fruition. We scored the first star just a few months after opening, along with eighteeen *Gault Millau* points. This not only filled me with satisfaction; it also proved that my radical focus on Asian flavors wasn't futile. But my increased fame meant a surprise was in store for me: It came in the form of a journalist from Berlin's *Tagesspiegel* newspaper who had been conducting research into a former teacher from the Hector Peterson high school, and had learned about my past with the *36 Boys*. When she mentioned it to me, I was momentarily lost for words — which doesn't happen very often. Of course I confirmed it to her; there was nothing to hide. I had never been ashamed of that phase of my life; it's just that no one had ever asked me about it. My days on the street had ended on my first trial day in the kitchen. Having to drop everything overnight is something that had been part of my life since childhood, when I had frequently moved to different cities and new environments.

My past with the *36 Boys*, which had all but disappeared out of my memory, was reappearing before me — and I was happy about it. I visited Muci, my old buddy, who was now a kickboxing world champion and ran a *36 Boys* shop in Kreuzberg. Even though we hadn't seen each other for twenty years, we were as close as ever. He was there in his tracksuit, and I with my cashmere scarf; but when you've fought side by side as we had, you shared an eternal bond like war veterans. He was pleased for me and my success; he knew how hard

2016
The quadriga on top of the Brandenburg Gate, Berlin's famous landmark

I had toiled to get where I had. And so it was that the bridge between Kottbusser Tor (the place with Berlin's highest crime rate) and the Brandenburg Gate (the place with the city's highest tourist rate) was built.

MA TIM RAUE was incredibly well received among the international guests in this part of Berlin. We quickly cemented the restaurant into the city's contemporary consciousness, and the awards attracted even more gourmets through our doors. I ironed out the final glitches — something my circumstances at 44 hadn't allowed. We no longer served bread and butter; our dishes were gluten- and lactose-free. The restaurant exuded an almost temple-like serenity, and in the open kitchen stood a much calmer head chef Tim Raue. There was no need to yell and scream, and we no longer had to fight to survive every day like we had at the SWISSÔTEL. At MA TIM RAUE, it was just about getting better. The strength and energy I had previously been forced to expend on facilitating hotel operations could now be fully focused on the plates. I had been served up the perfect environment; even the human resources aspect was back in my control. Just as I had promised, I gave my chefs more freedom and the opportunity to grow. Even the odd disappointment didn't veer me off my path of more liberal staff management. The hooligan in me was growing smaller, and just like it was being replaced by a more analytical side, so too was the basic cook being replaced by a more refined worker who focused increasingly on details. The paintball carnage was over, and in its place was a piece of machinery being oiled to make it better and better by the day.

But I still also cooked unconventional dishes at MA TIM RAUE, like veal tendons with pineapple and celery, whose gelatinous consistency was reminiscent of the tête de veau (veal brains) made popular by the top chefs of the 1980s and 1990s. I served fish maw, the swim bladder of fish, and abalone, a premium sea snail whose cooking time I had spent years trying to perfect. These ingredients and products worked wonderfully — in Hong Kong. But we were in Germany, and I couldn't see that I was forgetting about the guests who had made me famous and had always been loyal to me: the Berliners.

That wouldn't happen to me at the next stop on my journey: the RESTAURANT TIM RAUE, the quintessence of my work.

I had worked with Marie, my now ex-wife, since the early days of my career. We had met on the dance floor at a disco on the outskirts of Berlin in 1993. She was just about to complete her school-leaving exams at the time, while I had finished my second year as an apprentice chef. We had fallen in love and moved in together just a week later. While she had gone on to train as a restaurant management assistant, and progress to the position of restaurant manager very soon after, I had risen up the ranks to become first a chef and then head chef. We worked together at every restaurant whose service division fulfilled Marie's philosophy of professional but familiar guest relations. Sixteen-hour shifts were the norm for us. We worked hard for every success, and had to cope with the odd defeat over the years, but our strength lay in learning from our mistakes. We liked taking risks, no matter how tough, and in doing so pulled off the stunt of never losing our humor or killing the fun. When our visions ultimately diverged from those of MA TIM RAUE's owners in late 2009, she decided it was time to do our own thing: *It'll be expensive, but we'll manage it*. That was her view.

I wasn't exactly wild about the idea of swapping one of the country's highest paid chef jobs for a potential suicide mission, but

I had always trusted her in financial matters. Above all, we had had enough of owners who, sooner or later, ended up pursuing different interests to ourselves. Never again would anyone interfere with the setup or business operations. When a stroke of luck saw a lovely property in a grandiose old building on Kochstrasse (the present-day Rudi-Dutschke-Strasse) fall into our lap, we, in true old Raue fashion, managed to create in four months what would normally have required at least one or two years of planning.

Since then, RESTAURANT TIM RAUE has epitomized everything we stand for and consider important. The ambiance is less opulent than at MA TIM RAUE, but warmer and more detail-centered than 44, which was a rather puristic, almost neutral place. We didn't want floor-length tablecloths or candlesticks like something from King Louis XIV's court. I like graffiti, and am a huge admirer of Banksy. I love loud, bright colors and contrasting styles. Just as my dishes offer a burst of flavor no one expects, so the cabinet drawers at our restaurant reveal splashes of vivid pink. The interior combines timeless elegance with contemporary design. The fun side of my food is not muted by hunchback waiters, but is instead served by staff who celebrate typical Berliner casualness: never brash or irritatingly nonchalant; just friendly and highly professional.

When I left MA TIM RAUE, it was avant-garde to wear a black chef's jacket in the kitchen. I thought: *Berlin is blue, so we'll wear blue.* I felt so free I could have cooked in yellow underpants, and this freedom today still fills me with incredible pride on a daily basis. The restaurant is our life's work, which is why Marie and I still love working there every day — despite our personal split — to make each visit a unique experience for our guests.

RESTAURANT TIM RAUE is where I celebrate what I do best: translating existing dishes into extraordinary haute cuisine. The Wasabi Langoustine — my signature dish — is a perfect example of this. It's based on wasabi shrimp, a Cantonese dish I perfect by replacing the shrimp with a much juicier langoustine. The mayonnaise is made from real wasabi and Japanese mayo. I also increase the crispiness by sprinkling green Vietnamese rice flakes over the finished dish, and serve it with a Thai-inspired vinaigrette.

The plates are puristic, with no unnecessary embellishments, seeking instead to constantly provoke and inspire. What counts is the spectacle of flavors, the sum of the individual parts. I now know what I want; I'm aware of my presence and authority. I no longer have to test my limits. Previously, I had created dishes that were a deliberate challenge, a rollercoaster for the palate. Now, I combine flavors that are still a rollercoaster, but a controlled one. The ride is fun, not scary. I'm no longer walking the narrow tightrope between two buildings, with abysses on either side. My work comes from a feeling of peace and certainty, because I know what I stand for, and what I will continue to stand for in future. I make statements and don't wait for any epiphanies.

2016
East Side Gallery, Berlin

"I like graffiti, and am a huge admirer of Banksy. I love loud, bright colors and contrasting styles."

2016

In a sporty stance, Chinatown, Singapore

The blue chef's jacket is still my suit of armor, in which I focus on clearing away anything that causes problems. I've become freer, but not gentler, toward myself. Every day I fight with myself to improve both as a chef and a person. When my staff's strength wanes, I'm still the one who gives them that crucial boost which distinguishes winners from losers. The fact that many of my chefs have stuck with me for years also proves I've done something right in this respect. This continuity allows us to cook at our high level and to keep improving. These interactions, where knowledge is shared at every level and no one is left toiling away at their station with a tunnel-vision approach, are a critical factor in us being light years ahead of where we were when we first opened. They are what hoisted us into thirty-fourth place on the *World's 50 Best Restaurants* list in 2016, claiming the crown of Germany's best restaurant — an accolade beyond compare.

Our super-efficient processes mean we avoid the highly aggressive stress commonly found in kitchens. At the SWISSÔTEL, we slogged away like pigs, day in, day out, under the glaring neon lights. At RESTAURANT TIM RAUE, we turn the lights off during service time, and operate only using the spotlights at the individual stations. This calms the mind. We spend the entire day continuously preparing so that, by the evening, we're cruising. We briefly hit the throttle, but we're never really struggling. I also protect my chefs from this stress because I know what it can do to you. For example, I didn't notice that one of my most loyal chefs, who had been with me for years, was burned out, and I still berate myself for that to this day. My staff get three weeks' vacation during the summer. I make sure errors are analyzed clearly — through dialogue and much less foul language. I've become more precise in this area too. I explicitly tell people how I want things, and spare myself the aggravation. In many ways, I'm different to the reputation that still precedes me. People often expect a tattooed tyrant who can't string two sentences together, and who pelts his chefs with vegetables. They're puzzled

"Every day I fight with myself to improve both as a chef and a person."

when they instead encounter a direct but affable, articulate, and polite young man; it almost ends up being a bigger surprise than my dishes.

My team knows the liberties they can take — but they are also well aware what riles my old inner street fighter, who does not tolerate negligence. Due to the authority I have over my plates, however, I'm no longer just focused on myself. Like a yogi, I can stand at a station with my eyes closed and sense whether someone needs a break, or whether it's a day when someone lacks the will to give of their best and be a winner. I no longer have any thugs working the hotplates; instead, it's the Philipp Lahm (a German soccer player) generation. They know they only ever win or lose as a team. That's also why I mustn't be the only one showing off the shiny gold medal. I know my place. I know the areas in which I'm better than others — and that includes telling the world about our culinary feats in the kitchen.

What I won't be doing again is reducing the sweetness, sourness, or intensity of my cooking. I did that in the early years at RESTAURANT TIM RAUE as a way of following up my first star with a second. I toned things down by 15 percent, which was an important learning curve. Many guests started showing a level of enthusiasm I had never seen before. This "taming" had made my dishes easier to understand — but they still represented me. Taking out even more sweetness, sourness, and intensity — the holy trinity of my cooking — would mean renouncing everything I had achieved over the last few years. I can't do that, not even for the sake of a third star, despite declaring not so long ago that achieving a third star was my main aim. But I've learned not to be dogmatic about things, and to instead adapt when the situation requires it. The notion of evolution has fascinated me ever since my caravan hideout days in Bruchköbel. Evolution means further developing in order to survive. It's about adapting at the right moments in order to grow. Right from childhood, my life had always been about survival — not only physical, but also mental; to not fall by the wayside as a person. My cooking expresses my evolution, which is why it is like an art form for me. I conjure up the flavor combinations myself. You can't learn how to combine mango and violet, or tomato and galangal. You create it.

Since I can't go any higher, I've decided to go broader. At LA SOUPE POPULAIRE in Berlin, I'm continuing, at a high level, what I started at the KAISERSTUBEN: cooking typical Berlin dishes like

"Evolution means further developing in order to survive.

It's about adapting at the right moments in order to grow."

2016
Chinese dried goods store, with lots of new treasures for my kitchen, Chinatown, Singapore

2016
A view of my Lohberger-fitted kitchen at the Restaurant Tim Raue, just before lunch service

**"And if I do reopen the door,
I slam down a dish for the world as it
has never seen before:
Right into the gob, but with a bow."**

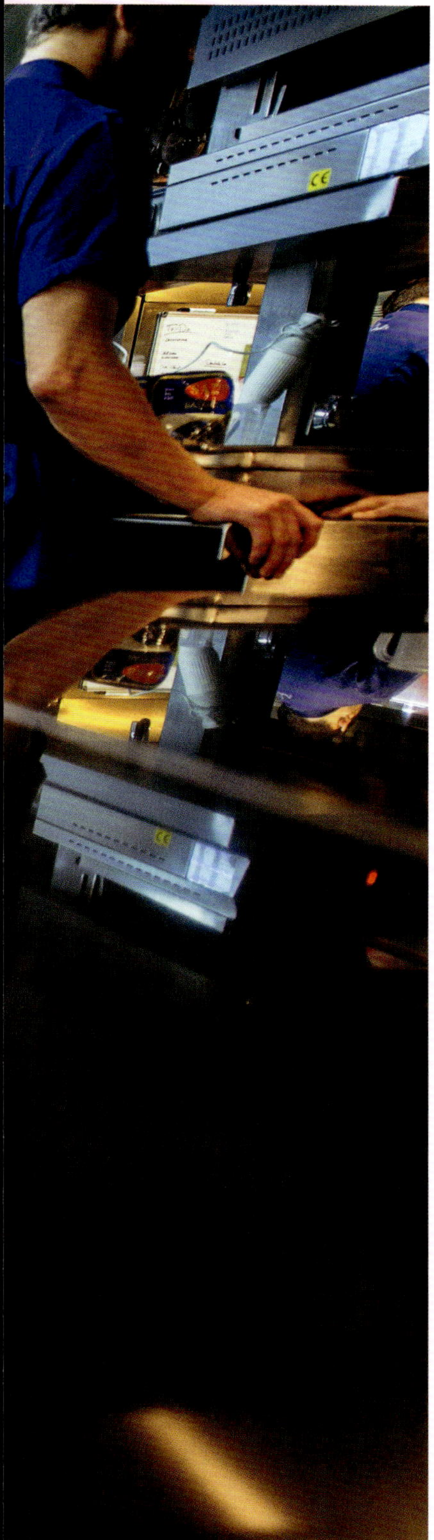

Königsberger Klopse (Königsberg meatballs) to superior but not elitist standards. And at BRASSERIE COLETTE, with restaurants in Berlin, Munich, and Constance, I'm reinterpreting the French bistro concept. I now know which projects work and which are a definite blow to the jaw.

I have reduced my dishes at RESTAURANT TIM RAUE, fine-tuning the essence of the ingredients. Five or six components don't make a course better; they may actually distort it. Three main components make it clearer and more precise. I broke out into a cold sweat leaving the wasabi marshmallows off my Wasabi Langoustine, but this ultimately refines the dish. You have to play with flavors, create contrasts. For years we've been cutting our scallops like sashimi and serving them with elderflower. But it was not until we added a touch of white onion puree that the thing really went off like a rocket.

I no longer have to fly around the world or wade through mountains of dishes to acquire these insights. All the flavors are within me. I don't need any external influences or sensory stimuli. While I travel because I enjoy being on the move, I have everything I need for my cooking in my head. I just need to give myself the opportunity to explore the dishes. This in turn requires isolation and moments of absolute peace. As such, I have learned to close the door behind me and decide how I use my time. I still live intensively every day, but no longer at the absolute limit, or with the worry that I could wake up the next day to find everything had been a dream and I was in fact lying in the gutter. My drive has remained the same, but something has come into my existence that means I have come to appreciate life.

And if I do reopen the door, I slam down a dish for the world as it has never seen before: right into the kissser, but with a bow.

Yours, Tim Raue

LOHBERGER

19

sam leong

"It was the culinary event that would change my career as a chef."

In 2004 I flew to Asia for the first time. As well as Bangkok and Hong Kong, I visited Singapore, where SWISSÔTELS & RAFFLES HOTELS, my then-employer, had its current headquarters.

With Marie, my then wife and today my business partner, I went for a meal at the JADE restaurant in the FULLERTON HOTEL. I had read in the *Wine & Dine Guide* that its young head chef was creating exciting dishes combining French ingredients, Western food presentation, and Chinese cooking. On the menu were amazing delicacies such as Peking Duck Skin with Foie Gras, Braised Ox Ribs with Cacao Jus and Raspberries, and, of course, the dish that was very fashionable at the time — Wasabi Shrimp. All of the dishes were outstanding in terms of their flavors; they surpassed our wildest expectations and catapulted me into a new dimension of tastes.

Everything, however, was outclassed by one particular dish, laconically named Baked Cod, Thai Mango Salad & Sweet-and-Sour Sauce. It was a crispy, steaming-hot piece of the very freshest, brilliantly white cod, topped with an ice-cold, Thai-spiced salad of green mangos, served with a piquant, typically Chinese, sweet-and-sour sauce. A rollercoaster of textures and temperatures, a play with hot, sweet, and sour. It was so magnificent that we immediately ordered the cod three more times.

The young head chef was Sam Leong, who was to become one of the most influential Singapore Chinese head chefs of all time. Only now, during some photo shoots in Singapore, was I able to meet him — my idol — in person. He is a wonderful man and a great chef, and I am eternally grateful to him for having revealed a new culinary world to me.

Following my first visit, I intensively studied the cuisines of Thailand, China, and Japan for three years, and developed the concept of how one day I wished to cook.

In 2008, at the RESTAURANT MA TIM RAUE, I started on the journey which I resolutely continued in 2010 at the RESTAURANT TIM RAUE. It took us into *The World's 50 Best Restaurants*, and gained us two stars in the *Michelin Guide*, nineteen *Gault Millau* points, as well as many other international awards, accolades, and distinctions.

2016
With Sam Leong outside his Forest restaurant (1* *Guide Michelin*) in Singapore. A farewell full of reverence on my part for one of the greatest Chinese chefs of today

2016
Wasabi Shrimp, Sam's signature dish

2016
Discussing new directions in modern Chinese cuisine with Chef Sam

andré chiang

„Ich hatte in meinem Leben stets Vorbilder und Menschen die mich inspiriert haben.“

Mein Idol als fußballbegeisterter Junge war Karl-Heinz Förster, ein knallharter Vorstopper, der für den VfB Stuttgart und die deutsche Nationalmannschaft spielte. Er war ein eleganter Spieler, mehr Gentleman als Hooligan, und so kompromisslos er auf dem Rasen war, so eloquent und sympathisch wirkte er außerhalb des Platzes. So wollte ich auch sein, und bis heute arbeite ich täglich daran.

Mit dem Beginn meiner Ausbildung und meinem Interesse für die besten Köche der damaligen Zeit trat Marco-Pierre White in mein Leben. Sein Kochbuch *White Heat* war meine Bibel. Es gibt darin ein Foto, auf dem der strubbelhaarige MPW mit einer Kippe im Mund eine Gänseleberterrine einsetzt. Das wirkte rebellisch und ultracool. Das Buch ist voller starker Sprüche von ihm, darunter *„Gott hat dir deine Hände nicht gegeben, damit du dir sie nicht verbrennst“*. Das fand ich grandios. Dann aß ich in seinem Restaurant OAK ROOM in London, und das Bild verpuffte. Der Kerl selbst wirkte echt geil, aber sein Essen war sterbenslangweilig.

Der Nächste in der Reihe war und ist Joachim Wissler aus dem VENDÔME. Er ist für mich der beste deutsche Koch, und das seit Langem. Niemand verbindet Modernität, akribisches Handwerk, Geschmack und stetigen Fleiß so wie er. Er schafft es, sich auf eine Sache, sein Restaurant, absolut zu fokussieren und jeden Tag daran zu arbeiten, es noch besser zu machen. Davor habe ich gewaltigen Respekt.

André traf ich das erste Mal persönlich vor drei Jahren anlässlich der *50-Best*-Gala in London. Wir stiegen auf der erweiterten Liste der Top-100-Restaurants auf Platz 78 ein, und ich wurde ihm vorgestellt. Dabei weiß ich schon seit 2007, wer er ist. Ich war noch beim SWISSÔTEL als Global Culinary Advisor beschäftigt, als mir vom Headquarter seine Unterlagen zugeschickt wurden. Er fing dann im Fine Dining Restaurant JAAN des SWISSÔTEL THE STANFORD in Singapur an und machte rasend schnell von sich reden. 2010 eröffnete er sein eigenes Restaurant in Singapur, das PAR ANDRÉ, und schaffte direkt den Sprung unter die *50 Best*.

André ist gebürtiger Taiwanese. Er verbrachte viele Jahre in den besten Küchen Frankreichs und kocht heute als Asiate französisch. Wenn man so will, spiegeln wir uns. Er ist sehr künstlerisch, und neben dem Fokus auf sein Fine Dining Restaurant betreibt er noch zwei Casual Restaurants. Mit ihm kann ich mich wunderbar austauschen, und er ist ein grandioser Kollege, der mich inspiriert.

Genau so, wie Singapur an sich für mich bis heute kulinarisch eine wichtige Inspirationsquelle ist und seit 2003 die Wurzel meines kulinarischen Turnarounds.

Live-Seafood-Aquarien im Long Beach Restaurant, Singapur

Frische Garnelen, Chinatown Market, Singapur

Getrocknete Abalonen, Chinatown Market, Singapur

Tim & André

Fish maw, Chinatown Market, Singapur

Frische Kalmare, Chinatown Market, Singapur

PART 03

recipes

starters & snacks

dim sum

fish

crustaceans & seafood

poultry

meat

desserts

basic recipes

For me, cooking is a wonderful way of to express yourself. You can combine skill and art, and live out your own individuality in the process.
Part of the skill is being able to perfectly fillet a fish, to cut carrots into diamond shapes, and to make dim sum.
The combination of ingredients and aromas and the creation of new dishes, are for me the artistic side.
Plating the food, which has such an exaggerated status in our visually oriented days, I consider an unimportant decorative detail. No one returns to a restaurant because the plates looked pretty.
Diners return if they've experienced unique moments of flavor, felt comfortable in terms of the ambience, and were attended during the meal by warm and welcoming servers.

But back to cooking.

________ The essence is, of course, to use only the very best, freshest, and finest ingredients. If you think you can just substitute, say, a frozen red fish (also known as the ocean perch) for the zander in my recipe and achieve an almost equivalent result, then you are simply wrong. For some of the ingredients, we've deliberately named the producers and suppliers to enable you to cook, for example, with Japanese products from Nishikidôri. If you want to take part in a Formula 1 race, then, as well as an extraordinary talent, you'll also need the right hardware. In our case, this means that without a Pacojet you'll find it hard to achieve the quality of frozen food from the demanding recipes. Our kitchen is today unimaginable without the Thermo-mix, which I discovered for myself only at a relatively late stage, although my cooks had been begging me for years to purchase one; now I know that no other machine produces such fine purees, powders, and jellies.

The Cook'n'Hold from Lohberger, who have superbly fitted out our entire kitchen, is a must-have for heating, keeping warm, and gently cooking meat, fish, poultry, and crustaceans. At home, it can be reasonably well replaced by a warming drawer, yet it's not quite the same. And without the ability to vacuumize, we would be unable to cook ingredients sous-vide, or to infuse vegetables in a marinade. The Excalibur dehydrates meringues at lightning speed and turns vegetables into chips.

If you want to be one of the best, you have to work with the best software and hardware. You have to be clear about the fact, therefore, that cooking a recipe in its entirety means an enormous amount of effort. But you can, of course, simply take individual components, such as sauces, pickled vegetables, purees, or vinaigrettes, and use them to complement your meals. The recipes are meant to inspire you, a thought-provoking impulse, and, if you like, a challenge.

All recipes, apart from the basic recipes, serve ten.

starters and snacks

We begin our menu with eight starters. Eight, because it is a lucky number in China, and because it fills the table with an abundance of small morsels. In aromatic terms, they are not as multidimensional as the subsequent courses, but instead they are aromatically placating plates, which burst with saltiness, heat, and acidity. They make your mouth water, and stoke anticipation for the subsequent dishes. You want to enjoy these with a second glass of Krug champagne.

In terms of dramatic composition, the first course in my menu concept is either a caviar dish, or one based around vegetables. It is meant to be a light entrance point, which instantly reveals the aromatics of our dishes.

In 2007, I redefined my philosophy and liberated my cuisine from French dogma, such as serving bread with every meal. The diners who come to our restaurants should not burden themselves with carbohydrates that are only ingested to satisfy their hunger. Instead, we serve larger portions of crustaceans, fish, poultry, and meat, and we give more space to vegetables and fruit. It is also the reason why there is no rice, no pasta, and no potatoes. This way, sweetness, acidity, heat, and the herbal aromas will be much more evident.

The dishes are less ambiguous in their taste and are not leveled out. We cook exclusively with lactose-free dairy products from the MinusL company. This means that our dishes are virtually lactose free, which makes them more easily digestible.

ZUCCHINI, MATCHA

In South Korea, during the Seoul Gourmet Festival, I enjoyed some amazing zucchini. They had absolutely nothing in common with the insipid vegetables I had previously encountered. I was thrilled by their crunchiness and sweetness. They had a wonderfully bitter aroma, which reminded me of tonic water. And this is what inspired me to create this appetizer, deliciously refreshing when enjoyed with a G&T mixed from Reisetbauer's Blue Gin and Fentimans Tonic.

ZUCCHINI:

10 SMALL, FIRM ZUCCHINI,
C. 3¼ × 1¼ IN (8 × 3 CM)
1½ CUPS (350 ML) RICE VINEGAR
3 PICKLED JALAPEÑO PEPPERS
7 TBSP (100 ML) JALAPEÑO MARINADE

Cut the zucchini lengthways into ¼ in (5 mm) slices.
Blend the rice vinegar, jalapeño peppers, and marinade in a Thermomix and strain through a fine-mesh strainer. Put the zucchini slices into a vacuum bag and pour over the liquid. Vacuumize and let infuse for 3 hours.
Take out the zucchini slices. Roll the slices around your little finger, then stand them up as rolls.

MATCHA FOAM:

1 CUP (250 G) YOGURT
14 TBSP (200 ML) GRANNY SMITH APPLE JUICE
7 TBSP (100 G) HEAVY CREAM
3½ TBSP (50 ML) LIME JUICE
4 TBSP (60 ML) GREEN CHILI SAUCE, STRAINED (→ SEE BASIC RECIPES)
2 TBSP (30 ML) TABASCO GREEN PEPPER SAUCE
5 TBSP (30 G) MATCHA TEA POWDER

Stir all the ingredients together, then lightly beat in a KitchenAid. Strain through a fine-mesh strainer and pour into an iSi soda siphon. Fit the siphon with two cream chargers.

GARNISH:

MATCHA TEA POWDER, FOR DUSTING

CUCUMBER & GARLIC

There is a cucumber salad in Sichuan cuisine, which features enormous amounts of garlic, a little vinegar, and some cucumber. This salad is extremely popular at Tian Fu, my favorite Sichuan restaurant in Berlin. Each time I tried a little of the salad I had to drink lots of wine afterwards to clear my palate. In our version we have reduced the amount of garlic significantly; however, this appetizer is also meant to encourage our guests to drink.

CUCUMBER:

4 CUCUMBERS
1¼ **CUPS (300 ML)** RICE VINEGAR
7 TBSP (100 ML) CHILI OIL
2 CUPS PLUS 1½ TBSP (500 ML) CUCUMBER JUICE
3 TBSP (45 ML) TABASCO GREEN PEPPER SAUCE
6 TBSP (90 ML) GREEN CHILI SAUCE (→ SEE BASIC RECIPES)
1 CUP PLUS 1½ TBSP (200 G) MUSCOVADO SUGAR
2½ TBSP (10 G) AGAR AGAR POWDER

Halve the cucumbers lengthways, then cut into ½ in (1.5 cm) slices. Combine the rice vinegar and the chili oil, add the cucumber slices, and vacuumize everything. Let infuse for 24 hours. Strain off the liquid, then combine in a saucepan with the cucumber juice, Tabasco, chili sauce, and sugar; bring to a boil.
Stir the agar agar powder into the boiling liquid and simmer for 5 minutes. Transfer the mixture to a bowl and let cool. Process in a Thermomix to a smooth jelly.

GARNISH:

GARLIC CHIPS (→ SEE BASIC RECIPES)

IMPERIAL CAVIAR, SPRATS & YUZU

For me, visiting a gourmet restaurant means that I can enjoy foods that I do not normally eat. This does, of course, include luxury products like white and black truffles, fish maw, and abalone in Cantonese eateries, toro and Kagoshima beef in Japanese kitchens, and in our own restaurant I would expect to find imperial caviar on the menu!

SPRAT MERINGUE:

1 LB 1½ OZ (500 G) SPRATS, PUREED
2 CUPS PLUS 1½ TBSP (500 ML) DASHI (→ SEE BASIC RECIPES)
8 CUPS (2 L) WATER
½ CUP PLUS 1½ TBSP (50 G) EGG WHITE POWDER
A TRACE OF XANTHAN GUM

Put the sprats, dashi, and water into a saucepan and simmer for 90 minutes, then strain the liquid through a cheesecloth. In a KitchenAid, whisk 14 tablespoons (200 ml) of the liquid together with the egg white powder and the xanthan until the mixture resembles a meringue mix. Transfer to a pastry bag with a round tip and pipe round disks of ¾ in (2 cm) diameter onto a Silpat baking mat. Dehydrate in an Excalibur Dehydrator for 12 hours at 149 °F (65 °C).

SPRAT BUTTERCREAM:

1 STICK PLUS 1 TBSP (½ CUP/125 G) SOFTENED SALTED BUTTER
2 TBSP (30 ML) PUREED SPRATS
1 ESPRESSO SPOON (2.5 ML) CHEF SAUCE (→ SEE BASIC RECIPES)

Using a whisk, beat the butter until foamy, then flavor to taste with the sprat puree and the chef sauce. Transfer the cream to a pastry bag with a small round tip and store at room temperature.

GARNISH:

FOR EACH PERSON ...
2 TSP (10 G) IMPERIAL CAVIAR
2 STALKS SORREL
2 DOTS OF YUZU MARMALADE (→ SEE BASIC RECIPES)
2 DOTS OF GREEN CHILI GEL (→ SEE BASIC RECIPES)
2 SMALL PIECES OF YUZU PEEL, CUT OUT AS DISKS
2 PIECES OF ICEBERG LETTUCE, CUT OUT AS DISKS ½ **IN (1.5 CM)** IN DIAMETER

AVOCADO, FINGER LIME & ALMOND MILK

This dish, which hails from my time at the Restaurant Ma Tim Raue in the Adlon Hotel, is a wonderfully summery starter. The current version is characterized by the interplay of ice-cold creaminess and acidity — exactly right for days when the thermometer rises above 100 °F (30 °C) outdoors.

AVOCADO FOAM:

5 AVOCADOS, PEELED AND PITTED
7 TBSP (100 ML) MUSHI SAUCE, STRAINED
(→ SEE BASIC RECIPES)
7 TBSP (100 ML) RICE VINEGAR
3½ TBSP (50 ML) GREEN CHILI SAUCE
(→ SEE BASIC RECIPES)
3½ TBSP (50 ML) ROSE'S LEMON CORDIAL
3½ TBSP (50 ML) MILK
2 TBSP (30 ML) TABASCO GREEN PEPPER SAUCE
CORNISH SEA SALT

In a Thermomix, process all the ingredients to a smooth mixture. Strain through a strainer and transfer to an iSi soda siphon. Fit the siphon with two cream chargers, shake well, and chill for 2 hours.

POMELO INFUSION:

1 POMELO
3 FINGER LIMES

Peel and segment the pomelo. Divide the flesh into suprêmes, juice the skins. Combine the suprêmes with the juice. Divide the finger limes into suprêmes and add to the pomelo.

ALMOND MILK ICE CREAM:

2 CUPS (500 G) YOGURT
½ CUP (120 G) ALMOND MILK
2 TBSP PLUS 1 TSP (35 ML) LIME JUICE
¼ CUP (80 G) GLUCOSE
1¼ OZ (30 G) BASIC TEXTUR
A PINCH OF CORNISH SEA SALT

Process all the ingredients in a Thermomix for 1 minute on Speed 4. Transfer the mixture to a Pacojet beaker and freeze overnight. Pacotize 1 hour before serving and freeze again.

ALMOND MILK MERINGUE:

14 TBSP (200 ML) WATER
7 TBSP (100 ML) CALPICO
1 TBSP PLUS 1 TSP (20 ML) ALMOND SYRUP
¾ CUP PLUS 2 TSP (75 G) EGG WHITE POWDER

Whisk all the ingredients in a KitchenAid to make a meringue mix. Transfer the mixture into a pastry bag, then pipe circular disks of ¾ in (2 cm) diameter onto a Silpat baking mat. Dehydrate overnight in an Excalibur Dehydrator at 131 °F (55 °C).

GARNISH:

FOR EACH PERSON ...
5 STEMS PERSINETTE® CRESS
3 SLICES HEARTS OF PALM, ¼ IN (5 MM) THICK
1 TBSP (15 ML) PARSLEY DRESSING
(→ SEE BASIC RECIPES)
1 SLICE OF PICKLED JALAPEÑO PEPPER, FINELY CHOPPED

FOIE GRAS, JIAOGULAN & MATCHA

In the 1990s, foie gras was an absolute must in gourmet restaurants, whether fried or as a terrine. Now that sophisticated cooking in Germany has emancipated itself from French haute cuisine, it is found less frequently. So as not to lapse into old French clichés — serving the liver with sweet fruits — we've created a dish that interweaves foie gras with herbal, bitter, and very complex aromas.

FOIE GRAS:

2 LB 3¼ OZ (1 KG) FOIE GRAS, VEINS AND MEMBRANES REMOVED, AND DICED
1 TBSP (15 ML) PICKLING SALT
1 TBSP (6 G) MATCHA TEA POWDER

Sprinkle 7 oz (200 g) of the foie gras with pickling salt and matcha powder, then process in a Thermomix to a smooth mixture. Gently fold in the remaining goose liver dice. Transfer the mixture onto a large sheet of plastic wrap and roll up, closing the ends well. Now tightly wrap the plastic wrap roll in aluminum foil. Cook the foie gras in a bain-marie for 20 minutes at 113 °F (45 °C), then plunge into iced water. Let the foie gras cool completely so it sets, then cut into ½ in (1.5 cm) slices.

GRAPE GEL:

1⅔ CUPS (400 ML) VAN NAHMEN'S RIESLING GRAPE JUICE
7 TBSP (100 ML) ROSE'S LEMON CORDIAL
1¼ TSP (5 G) AGAR AGAR POWDER

In a saucepan, combine the grape juice and the lemon cordial and bring to a boil. Stir in the agar agar powder and simmer for 5 minutes. Transfer the mixture to a Thermomix bowl and let cool. Process to a smooth mixture, then transfer into a spray bottle.

GRAPES:

1 LB 1½ OZ (500 G) SEEDLESS GRAPES
14 TBSP (200 ML) VAN NAHMEN'S RIESLING GRAPE JUICE
7 TBSP (100 ML) ROSE'S LEMON CORDIAL

Vacuumize all the ingredients in a bag, chill and let infuse for 12 hours. Remove the grapes and place them on a Silpat baking mat. Dehydrate in a Rational CombiMaster for 4 hours at 185 °F (85 °C) (convection).

NORI TOAST:

¾ CUP (180 G) EGG YOLK
½ CUP PLUS 2 TBSP (150 G) EGG WHITE
⅔ CUP PLUS ⅔ TBSP (160 G) SUGAR
3½ TBSP (50 G) LIQUID BUTTER
3 TBSP (50 G) GLUTEN-FREE FLOUR
1 TBSP (6 G) MATCHA TEA POWDER
1 TBSP (0.5 G) NORI SEAWEED POWDER
CLARIFIED BUTTER FOR FRYING

Stir together all the ingredients and set aside for 15 minutes to swell. Transfer to an iSi soda siphon and fit the siphon with two cream chargers. Squirt the mixture into a square GN-1/6 container and cook in a microwave for 25 seconds. Let cool, then slice and cut out circles of 1½ in (4 cm) diameter. Fry the seaweed toasts on both sides in clarified butter.

GARNISH:

FOR EACH PERSON ...
3 JIAOGULAN LEAVES
3 NORI SEAWEED LEAVES, **¼ × ¼ IN (5 × 5 MM)**
¼ OZ (5 G) NISHIKIDÔRI MARKET'S FRESH WASABI

ASPARAGUS & WOODRUFF

When I think of asparagus, I'm inevitably reminded of the 600 lb (240 kg) or so I had to prepare as a chef in my younger days — every single day. For my first two years I was apprenticed to an upmarket day-trip excursion restaurant, and during the asparagus season we had to stand and peel the stems in the kitchen for 12 hours at a trot, our lower arms covered in plastic wrap and our hands in ski gloves for protection. Since then, I've not been a great fan of asparagus, and that's not even been changed by this wonderful asparagus dish.

ASPARAGUS:

2 LB 3¼ OZ (1 KG) WHITE ASPARAGUS
8 CUPS (2 L) WATER
1 CUP PLUS 1½ TBSP (200 G) MUSCOVADO SUGAR
2 TBSP (20 G) CORNISH SEA SALT
4 TBSP (60 ML) ELDERFLOWER SYRUP
5 TBSP (80 ML) RICE VINEGAR
CORNISH SEA SALT
XANTHAN GUM

Peel the asparagus stems and cut off ⅜ in (1 cm) ends.
Make the broth. In a saucepan, bring to a boil the cut-off asparagus ends with the water, sugar, salt, and elderflower syrup. Simmer for 15 minutes, then strain the broth through a cheesecloth. Set aside the asparagus ends.
In a shallow saucepan, bring the liquid to a boil again. Add the asparagus spears, bring back to a boil, then simmer until the asparagus is firm to the bite but not yet completely cooked. Remove the asparagus, wrap to a moistened cloth to cool, then cut into 1½ in (4 cm) lengths.
In a Thermomix, puree the cooked asparagus ends with the rice vinegar and season with salt. Thicken the mixture with a little xanthan so it has a jelly-like consistency.

WOODRUFF DRESSING:

½ LETTUCE
HALF A HANDFUL OF FRESH WOODRUFF
½ CUP (100 G) SUGAR
3 TBSP (15 ML) MUSTARD
1 CUP (250 ML) DASHI
(→ SEE BASIC RECIPES)
1 CUP (250 ML) RICE VINEGAR
XANTHAN GUM
4 TBSP PLUS 2 TSP (75 ML) LEMON OIL
(→ SEE BASIC RECIPES)
11 TBSP PLUS 2 TSP (175 ML) VEGETABLE OIL
WOODRUFF SYRUP
YUZU JUICE
GREEN CHILI SAUCE (→ SEE BASIC RECIPES)

Very finely chop the lettuce and the woodruff. Puree with the sugar, mustard, dashi, and rice vinegar in a Thermomix and thicken lightly with several pinches of xanthan.
Combine the two oils and gradually add to the lettuce and woodruff mixture in the Thermomix at Speed 3.
Season the dressing with woodruff syrup, yuzu juice, and chili sauce.

GARNISH:

FOR EACH PERSON ...
3 DOTS JALAPEÑO GEL
3 STRIPS ROMAINE LETTUCE
3 WOODRUFF LEAVES
2 BELLIS FLOWERS

SCALLOPS, ELDERFLOWERS & THAI PEPPERCORNS

This scallop dish will probably soon feature as one of the great classics of our cuisine. We prepared them at food symposia in Asia, Europe, and the Middle East, and during the Graz Chefdays we dispatched them from the stage to 500 people — all the guests who were present. However, it's not the scallops that are in the foreground here but the elderflower stock, which, I think, is an impressive representative of my intensely aromatic dishes.

SCALLOPS:

16 FRESH SCALLOPS
1 CUP PLUS 2 TBSP (200 G) SUGAR
2½ CUPS (400 G) CORNISH SEA SALT
1 ESPRESSO SPOON (2.5 ML) GROUND WHITE PEPPER

Open the shells, separate out the meat and free it from the coral and the beards. Place in iced water for 1 hour.
Combine the sugar, salt, and pepper. Sprinkle one-third of the mixture onto a baking sheet, place the scallops on top, then cover with the remaining mixture and dry-cure for 30 minutes. Remove the scallops and wash off the spices. Place the scallops onto a baking sheet and steam in a Rational CombiMaster for 3 minutes at 180 °F (82 °C). Take the scallops out of the steamer and plunge them into iced water. Transfer onto paper towels and pat dry. Cut each scallop into three slices.

ELDERFLOWER BROTH:

1⅓ CUPS (300 ML) RICE VINEGAR
14 TBSP (200 ML) ELDERFLOWER SYRUP
7 TBSP (100 ML) ROSE'S LEMON CORDIAL
3½ TBSP (50 ML) GREEN CHILI SAUCE, STRAINED (→ SEE BASIC RECIPES)
4 TBSP (60 ML) TABASCO GREEN PEPPER SAUCE
XANTHAN GUM

In a Thermomix, blend all the ingredients apart from the xanthan for 2 minutes on Speed 10, then thicken lightly with several pinches of xanthan.

PRESERVED APPLES, MELONS & CUCUMBERS:

16 SLICES OF PINK LADY APPLE, CUT OUT WITH A CUTTER
7 TBSP (100 ML) PINK LADY APPLE JUICE

Vacuumize both ingredients together and let infuse for 1 hour.

16 SLICES OF GALIA MELON, CUT OUT WITH A CUTTER
7 TBSP (100 ML) GALIA MELON JUICE

Vacuumize both ingredients together and let infuse for 1 hour.

16 SLICES OF CUCUMBER, CUT OUT WITH A CUTTER
7 TBSP (100 ML) CUCUMBER JUICE

Vacuumize both ingredients together and let infuse for 1 hour.

GARNISH:

FOR EACH PERSON ...
3 FRESH GREEN THAI PEPPERCORNS, HALVED
½ ESPRESSO SPOON (1.25 ML) VERY FINELY CHOPPED LEMONGRASS
3 HEARTLEAF ICEPLANT LEAVES
3 STEMS WILD CHERVIL
3 DOTS OF WHITE ONION CREAM (→ SEE BASIC RECIPES)

CELTUCE & GILT-HEAD BREAM

Celtuce, whose German name translates as Chinese drumstick, suits our cooking style. For this variety of lettuce you don't eat the leaves but the stem. This has a deliciously crunchy texture, but it does need to be well peeled and always has to be cooked. In this recipe, it gives the bream sashimi added freshness and texture.

CELTUCE:

1¼ CUPS (300 ML) RICE VINEGAR
10 TBSP (150 ML) ELDERFLOWER SYRUP
3½ TBSP (50 ML) ROSE'S LEMON CORDIAL
3½ TBSP (50 ML) LIME JUICE
2 STEMS CELTUCE (ASPARAGUS LETTUCE), PEELED

Combine the liquid ingredients and vacuumize together with the two celtuce stems. Steam in a Rational CombiMaster for 1 hour at 180 °F (82 °C). Let the stems cool, then cut into ¼ in (5 mm) slices with an electric slicer.

BREAM SASHIMI:

3 CUPS (500 G) CORNISH SEA SALT
2¼ CUPS (500 G) WHITE SUGAR
2 TBSP (60 ML) GROUND WHITE PEPPER
10 GILT-HEAD BREAM FILLETS, SKINS AND BONES REMOVED

Combine the salt, sugar, and white pepper. Sprinkle some of the mixture onto a baking sheet, place the bream fillets on top, and cover with the remaining mixture. Chill for 20 minutes. Wash the bream fillets, pat dry, then cut like sashimi.

TAPIOCA:

14 TBSP (200 ML) GRANNY SMITH APPLE JUICE
7 TBSP (100 ML) ROSE'S LEMON CORDIAL
2 TBSP (60 ML) TABASCO GREEN PEPPER SAUCE
XANTHAN GUM
⅔ CUP (100 G) SMALL GREEN TAPIOCA PEARLS, COOKED

Stir together the apple juice, lemon cordial, and Tabasco and thicken lightly with a little xanthan. Stir in the tapioca pearls and let infuse for 3 hours.

GARNISH:

FOR EACH PERSON …
5 PEARL ONION QUARTERS
1 ESPRESSO SPOON (2.5 ML) FURIKAKE POWDER
3 DOTS OF JALAPEÑO GEL (→ SEE BASIC RECIPES)
3 HEARTLEAF ICEPLANT LEAVES
2 TRACES OF WAKAME POWDER
3 STRIPS OF LEMON ZEST

CELERY ROOT, ONION & TRUFFLE

My long-standing chef, Christian Singer, comes from Swabia, and at times displays flashes of his culinary origins. His cheese spaetzle for the staff lunch are unrivalled, and his way of dealing with such a simple ingredient as the onion was the inspiration for this dish. He cooked an onion soup that was so fragrant and elegant that we decided to use it as the base for a new dish. The soup contains celery root, our starting point, which we turned into this ravishing and complexly flavored starter demanding a high degree of craftsmanship.

CELERY ROOT:

2⅔ CUPS (400 G) CELERY ROOT, PEELED AND DICED
2 TBSP (30 G) LEE KUM KEE CHAR SIU SAUCE
1 TBSP (20 G) HONEY
1 TSP (3 ML) CORNISH SEA SALT
7 TBSP (100 G) JAPANESE MAYONNAISE
1 CUP (70 G) BLACK WINTER TRUFFLE BREAKINGS
1 TBSP PLUS 1 TSP (20 G) RED CHILI SAUCE, STRAINED (→ SEE BASIC RECIPES)
1 TBSP PLUS 1 TSP (20 G) MUSHI SAUCE, STRAINED (→ SEE BASIC RECIPES)
3½ TBSP (50 ML) MARSALA
7 TBSP (100 ML) APPLE JUICE
10 SLICES OF PINK LADY APPLE, **2½ × 2 IN (6 × 5 CM)**

In a bowl, marinate the celery root dice in the char siu sauce, honey, and salt. Wrap the celery root in baking paper, place in a deep baking pan, and cover with a baking sheet. Cook in the oven for 2 hours at 284 °F (140 °C). Let cool, then roughly chop.
Combine the mayonnaise, truffles, and both sauces with the celery root and transfer the mixture to a pastry bag. Fit the bag with a round tip of ¾ in (2 cm) in diameter.
Bring the marsala to a boil with the apple juice, then let cool. Vacuumize the apple slices with the liquid and let infuse for 1 hour. Take out of the liquid and place a little of the celeriac mixture onto each apple slice.

LETTUCE COMPOTE:

3 HEADS OF LETTUCE
CORNISH SEA SALT
3 TBSP (45 ML) YUZU MARMALADE (→ SEE BASIC RECIPES)
3 TBSP (45 ML) GREEN CHILI SAUCE (→ SEE BASIC RECIPES)
2 TSP (10 ML) TABASCO GREEN PEPPER SAUCE
1 TSP (5 ML) LIME JUICE

Finely chop the lettuce and briefly blanch in salted water, then gently squeeze out. Flavor the lettuce mixture with the remaining ingredients. Shape the mixture into quenelles.

ONION SOUP:

10 CUPS (1.5 KG) PEELED AND SLICED WHITE ONIONS
1 CELERY ROOT, PEELED AND DICED
3 QUARTS PLUS ¾ CUP (3 L) DUCK BROTH (→ SEE BASIC RECIPES)

Wrap the onion and the celery root in baking paper and cook in the oven at 356 °F (180 °C) until the vegetables are dark brown.
In a saucepan, bring the duck broth to a boil. Add the roasted vegetables and simmer for 2 hours, then strain through a cheesecloth.

HAZELNUT MAYONNAISE:

7 TBSP (100 G) JAPANESE MAYONNAISE
2 TBSP (30 G) HAZELNUT PASTE
1 TBSP PLUS 1 TSP (20 ML) TRUFFLE JUICE

Stir together all the ingredients.

GARNISH:

FOR EACH PERSON …
3 DOTS HAZELNUT MAYONNAISE
2 JAPANESE RICE CRACKERS
2 BLOCKS OF KARANGSARI SAMBAL PECEL, **¼ × ¼ IN (5 × 5 MM)**
3 STEMS OF CHICKWEED
3 SLICES OF BLACK WINTER TRUFFLE, CUT OUT AS SLICES OF **¾ IN (2 CM)** IN DIAMETER

BRUSSELS SPROUTS, BANANA & LIME

Walking through the kitchen and randomly trying what is at that moment being produced or cooked in the various departments, brings about unique new flavor combinations again and again. In this particular case, I tried some banana mousse from the patissier and the next moment some cooked Brussels sprouts from the entremetier — and, voilà, an extraordinary aroma developed on the palate.
The banana imbued the sprouts with delicate and elegant traits, and the hearty cabbage flavor was noticeably weakened. Last winter, it resulted in this vegetable dish, which was exceptionally well received by our guests.

BRUSSELS SPROUTS:

11⅓ CUPS (1 KG) BRUSSELS SPROUTS
CORNISH SEA SALT

Carefully remove the outer leaves of the sprouts. Blanch the outer leaves briefly in salted water and set aside. (They are later briefly blanched and filled, then reassembled so as to look like complete sprouts.)
Cook the sprout hearts in salted water until very soft.

BRUSSELS SPROUTS CREAM:

⅔ CUP (150 G) FINELY DICED BACON
1 CUP (150 G) PEELED AND FINELY DICED ONIONS
3½ TBSP (50 ML) HEAVY CREAM
3½ TBSP (50 ML) LIQUID BUTTER
3 TBSP (45 ML) GREEN CHILI SAUCE
(→ SEE BASIC RECIPES)
1 TBSP (15 ML) GARLIC OIL
(→ SEE BASIC RECIPES)
2 TBSP (30 ML) SMOKED OIL
(→ SEE BASIC RECIPES)

In a skillet or frying pan, fry the bacon, then add the onion, and sauté in the fat. In a Thermomix, process the cooked sprouts (SEE ABOVE), the bacon and onion mixture, and the remaining ingredients to a smooth mixture.

BANANA MOUSSE:

2 BANANAS
1 TBSP (15 ML) VERY FINELY CHOPPED LEMONGRASS
1 TSP (5 ML) VERY FINELY CHOPPED LIME LEAVES
JUICE OF ½ LIME

Mash the bananas with a fork, then combine them with the remaining ingredients.
Place the banana mousse and the sprout cream onto the outer sprout leaves, and shape into round Brussels sprouts.

LIME SAUCE:

1 CUP (250 ML) LIME JUICE
½ CUP (125 ML) GREEN CHILI SAUCE
(→ SEE BASIC RECIPES)
½ CUP (125 ML) ROSE'S LEMON CORDIAL
XANTHAN GUM

Stir together the lime juice, chili sauce, and lemon cordial and lightly thicken with a little xanthan.

WILD JUNGLE PEANUTS:

¾ CUPS PLUS 2 TBSP (200 G) THAI YELLOW CURRY PASTE
3½ TBSP (50 ML) VEGETABLE OIL
4½ CUPS (1 L) WATER
2¼ CUPS (500 G) SUGAR
1⅓ CUPS (250 G) MUSCOVADO SUGAR
4 CUPS (600 G) WILD JUNGLE PEANUTS

In a saucepan, lightly sauté the curry paste in the vegetable oil. Add the remaining ingredients apart from the peanuts, and cook everything to a syrupy mixture.
Stir the peanuts into the mixture to marinate. Place on a Silpat baking mat and dehydrate in an Excalibur Dehydrator for 12 hours at 158 °F (70 °C).

GARNISH:

FOR EACH PERSON …
1 TSP (5 ML) SMOKED OIL
(→ SEE BASIC RECIPES)
4 STEMS CILANTRO SPROUTS

RADISHES, RIND & MISO MAYO

The best snack in the world to enjoy while watching a soccer match! Crispy, salty, sweet-and-sour crunchy, and with a fatty umami flavor. Washed down with a jeroboam bottle of dry white Einzigacker Cuvée from the Dreissigacker vineyard in Germany — and kick off.

PORK RIND:

7 OZ (200 G) RIND OF CURED AND COOKED PORK BELLY
6½ CUPS (1.5 L) WATER
2 CUPS PLUS 1½ TBSP (500 ML) DASHI
(→ SEE BASIC RECIPES)
FAT FOR DEEP-FRYING

Simmer the pork, water, and dashi in a sauté pan for 90 minutes. Take out the rind and cut it into 2 × ⅜ in, (5 × 1 cm) strips. Place them on a Silpat baking mat and dehydrate in an Excalibur Dehydrator for 12 hours at 140 °F (60 °C). Deep-fry the rind in fat at 392 °F (200 °C). Place onto paper towels and pat dry.

RADISHES:

10½ OZ (300 G) RADISHES
½ CUP (125 ML) MUSHI SAUCE
(→ SEE BASIC RECIPES)
7 TBSP (100) ML RICE VINEGAR
1 TBSP PLUS 2 TSP (25 ML) ROSE'S LEMON CORDIAL

Cut the radishes into ⅜ in (1 cm) slices. Bring all the liquids together to a boil, add the radishes, bring back to a boil, and simmer for 1 minute. Strain off the liquid and reserve, let the liquid and the radishes cool. Vacuumize the radishes and the liquid together and let infuse for 24 hours.

MISO MAYO:

10 TBSP (150 G) JAPANESE MAYONNAISE
3½ TBSP (50 G) WHITE MISO PASTE
2 TSP (10 G) SMOKED OIL
(→ SEE BASIC RECIPES)

Stir together all the ingredients.

GARNISH:

1 STEM OF ACLLA CRESS® FOR EACH RADISH

BRUSSELS SPROUTS, DASHI & YUZU

This dish is one of our typical appetizers, one of a total of eight, which we serve as soon as our guests sit down. These appetizers are predominantly one-dimensional in flavor, boldly and very strongly, perhaps even a little excessively spiced, in this case salty with a hint of sweetness and intense cabbage aromas. So there's nothing you can do but to refresh yourself with a glass of Krug Grande Cuvée champagne!

BRUSSELS SPROUTS:

30 SMALL BRUSSELS SPROUTS
FAT FOR DEEP-FRYING
CORNISH SEA SALT

Blanch the Brussels sprouts for 3 minutes, then immediately plunge them into iced water. Separate out the leaves and remove every second layer so that the hot fat can penetrate between the layers during deep-frying. Deep-fry the sprouts for about 1 minute in fat heated to 356 °F (180 °C). Drain on kitchen paper, pat dry, and season with salt to taste.

DASHI GEL:

14 TBSP (200 ML) DASHI
(→ SEE BASIC RECIPES)
7 TBSP (100 ML) ROSE'S LEMON CORDIAL
1 TSP (3 G) AGAR AGAR POWDER

Combine the dashi and the lemon cordial and bring to a boil, stir in the agar agar, and simmer for 5 minutes. Transfer the mixture to a Thermomix bowl and let cool. Process to a smooth gel and transfer to a spray bottle.

GARNISH:

FOR EACH PERSON ...
3 DOTS OF YUZU MARMALADE
(→ SEE BASIC RECIPES)
3 PINCHES OF EXTRA FINE BONITO FLAKES

COLETTE VINTAGE SARDINES, LIME & TOAST

Sometimes, if there is an excellent product, you don't actually have to cook much. In fact, these vintage sardines, which we obtain from Maître Philippe in Berlin for the three Colette Tim Raue Brasseries, only need a little piece of grilled sourdough bread and a lime quarter. The Colette Brasseries, which are based at the Tertianum Premium Residences in Constance, Munich, and Berlin, offer a contemporary French brasserie cuisine. I created the dishes together with my long-standing former head chef, Steve Karlsch, the present culinary director of the Tertianum Premium Residences and the Colette Brasseries, and with our current head chef, Dominik Obermeier. Not all the recipes are as easy to cook for yourself as this one, but this is my favorite, to be enjoyed with a glass of Ermitage blanc by Chapoutier.

SARDINES & TOAST:

4 CANS OF LA PERLE DES DIEUX 2015 VINTAGE SARDINES
1 SLICE OF SOURDOUGH BREAD, ¾ **IN (2 CM)** THICK AND QUARTERED

Briskly broil the bread slices on both sides over a charcoal broiler.

GARNISH:

4 LIME QUARTERS

dim sum

Every time I arrive in Singapore or Hong Kong, I immediately go to the nearest dim sum restaurant. Happily, the range of dim sum dishes has increased enormously in the last few years.

Today, Chinese chefs are also very imaginative, creating new dim sum variations, something which for centuries was rather frowned upon.

The best dim sums, in my opinion, are served at Restaurant 8 in Macao. In terms of their aromas, they are as magnificent as those at the Lung King Heen in Hong Kong and the Tim Wan Ho in Singapore, and in design terms each one is a work of art.

Dim sums are a sin for us — they are the only dishes we prepare with wheat, rice, or tapioca flour. We therefore only serve them for lunch, so diners have a chance to work off the carbohydrates after the meal.

BAMBOO FUNGUS, SCALLOP MUSCLE & GINSENG

The bamboo fungus, known as "bamboo piths" in Hong Kong, has a unique, spongy texture. It absorbs the liquid in which it cooks, in our case a stock made from chicken and ginseng, refined with the acidity of limes and the heat of Combava chile from Mauritius. Bamboo piths are often filled and steamed in China; in this recipe, we use a combination of rich bone marrow and delicately nutty scallops.

DIM SUM:

20 BAMBOO FUNGI
1 LB 1½ OZ (500 G) SCALLOP MUSCLE, FINELY DICED
1 LB 1½ OZ (500 G) BEEF BONE MARROW, COOKED AND FINELY DICED
10½ OZ (300 G) CHICKEN STUFFING
(→ SEE BASIC RECIPES)
½ CUP (120 ML) NISHIKIDÔRI MARKET WASABI PASTE
½ CUP (120 ML) CHEF SAUCE
(→ SEE BASIC RECIPES)
CORNISH SEA SALT

Soak the fungi for 1 hour in lukewarm water. Halve the fungi, cutting the ends straight.
To make the filling, combine the scallop muscles, bone marrow, chicken stuffing, wasabi paste, and chef sauce in a bowl and season with Cornish sea salt.
Place 20 bamboo fungus pieces on separate 6 × 6 in (15 × 15 cm) squares of plastic wrap, put 1 tablespoon of filling on top and cover with a second piece of bamboo fungus.
Fold over the plastic wrap and twist together to make a parcel. Cook the parcels for 8 minutes in water heated to 185°F (85°C). Let cool, then remove the plastic wrap. Reheat the dim sum in a bamboo steamer before serving.

GINSENG BROTH:

4½ CUPS (1 L) CHICKEN BROTH
(→ SEE BASIC RECIPES)
2¼ OZ (6 G) GINSENG ROOTS
10 TBSP (150 ML) ROSE'S LEMON CORDIAL
2 TBSP (30 ML) COMBAVA CHILI PASTE
ZEST OF **3** LIMES
7 TBSP (100 ML) LIQUID BUTTER

In a saucepan, combine the chicken broth and the ginseng. Bring to a boil, then simmer for 30 minutes. Turn off the heat and let the broth infuse for 1 hour.
Remove the ginseng roots and set aside. Add all the remaining ingredients to the broth and bring back to a boil. Pour 5 tablespoons (80 ml) per person into each bowl.

GARNISH:

FOR EACH PERSON ...
2 SLICES GINSENG ROOT
4 COOKED CARROT BALLS
4 COOKED CELERY ROOT BALLS
4 SLICES SPRING LEEK, SAUTÉED IN A WOK
½ ESPRESSO SPOON (1.25 ML) BROCCOLI FLOWERS
PERSINETTE® CRESS

BRIOCHE, GOOSE & BLACK TRUFFLE

I grew up with classic French cuisine, and in France, goose foie gras is typically eaten with brioche. In dim sum cooking, a yeast dough is often used to make filled bread rolls. We've adopted this principle and added a typically Berlin component of deep-fried doughnuts. The result is a hot, oily, juicy dim sum, which is crowned with a generous amount of black truffle and crunchy Jerusalem artichoke.

BRIOCHE ROLLS:

14 TBSP (200 ML) MILK
1½ OZ (42 G) FRESH YEAST
5¼ CUPS (650 G) ALL-PURPOSE FLOUR
¼ CUP (50 G) SUGAR
5 EGGS
4 TBSP (60 G) LIQUID BUTTER
FAT FOR DEEP-FRYING

Heat the milk with the yeast until all the yeast has dissolved. Put the flour, sugar and eggs into a KitchenAid mixing bowl, add the milk and yeast mixture and stir together. Gradually pour the butter into the dough, stirring all the time. Let the dough rest for 30 minutes.
Roll out the dough to ½ in (1 cm) thick. Cut out circles of 3¼ in (8 cm) diameter, then pull them apart with both thumbs. Place 1½ oz (40 g) filling (SEE RIGHT) onto each dough circle, fold the dough over the filling and shape into a little ball. Let rise for 10 minutes. Heat the fat to 350 °F (180 °C) and deep-fry the balls in it until lightly browned.

FILLING:

1 LB 1½ OZ (500 G) GOOSE FOIE GRAS, FRIED, COOLED, AND DICED
4¼ OZ (120 G) GOOSE HEARTS, SAUTÉED AND DICED
8¾ OZ (250 G) CHICKEN STUFFING (→ SEE BASIC RECIPES)
⅓ CUP (100 G) LEE KUM KEE CHAR SIU SAUCE
5 TSP WANGSHOUYI THIRTEEN-SPICE POWDER
⅓ CUP (100 G) HONEY
CORNISH SEA SALT

Put all the ingredients into a bowl and stir to combine. Season with salt to taste.

HAZELNUT MAYONNAISE:

7 TBSP (100 G) JAPANESE MAYONNAISE
3½ TBSP (50 G) HAZELNUT PASTE
¼ CUP (20 G) ROASTED AND CRUSHED HAZELNUT KERNELS
1½ TBSP (20 ML) MUSHI SAUCE, STRAINED (→ SEE BASIC RECIPES)
CORNISH SEA SALT

Put all the ingredients into a bowl and stir to combine. Season with salt to taste.

JERUSALEM ARTICHOKE:

2⅔ CUPS (400 G) SLICED JERUSALEM ARTICHOKES, SHAVED INTO ⅛ **IN (3 MM)** SLICES
5 TBSP (80 ML) RICE VINEGAR

Marinate the Jerusalem artichoke slices in the rice vinegar.

GARNISH:

FOR EACH PERSON ...
1 TSP (4 G) BLACK WINTER TRUFFLE, COOKED AND CUT INTO THIN STRIPS
2 DOTS OF RED CHILI COMPOTE (→ SEE BASIC RECIPES)
1 ESPRESSO SPOON (2.5 ML) SHAVED HAZELNUT KERNELS, CARAMELIZED
1 STEM CHICKWEED

PORK, YUZU & MAYONNAISE

This recipe is relatively easy to follow, because even we use ready-made wonton pastry. Try to find Happy Boy wonton pastry; it should be available in well-stocked Asian stores. This pastry is as yellow as maize, and turns particularly juicy and tender after steaming. The recipe was one of our first dim sums, and it has since become a classic on the lunch menu.

WONTON:

1 (7 OZ/200G) PACKAGE HAPPY BOY WONTON PASTRY

Fill the wonton sheets with the filling mixture (SEE RIGHT) and steam in a Rational CombiMaster at 212 °F (100 °C). Now dry-fry the underside in a non-stick skillet or frying pan for 30 seconds.

FILLING:

14 OZ (400 G) PORK BELLY, CURED, COOKED, AND FINELY DICED
7 OZ (200 G) CHICKEN STUFFING (→ SEE BASIC RECIPES)
2 CUPS (100 G) PEELED AND FINELY DICED GINGER
⅓ CUP (80 G) THINLY SLICED SPRING LEEK
CORNISH SEA SALT
FRESHLY GROUND WHITE PEPPER
RED CHILI SAUCE (→ SEE BASIC RECIPES)

In a bowl, combine the pork belly, chicken stuffing, ginger, and spring leek, then season generously with salt, pepper, and chili sauce.

YUZU MAYONNAISE:

2 CUPS (500 G) JAPANESE MAYONNAISE
⅔ CUP (200 G) YUZU MARMALADE
2 TBSP (30 ML) TABASCO GREEN PEPPER SAUCE

Combine all the ingredients in a bowl.

GARNISH:

FOR EACH PERSON …
2 LEEK SLICES, STEAMED
1 TSP (5 ML) CHIVE OIL (→ SEE BASIC RECIPES)

SQUID TEMPURA, LETTUCE & LIME

Our dim sum menu includes a dish that originated in Japanese tempura cuisine. The inspiration was battered and deep-fried squid, which I enjoyed during my first visit to Japan in a *Michelin*-starred tempura restaurant. I'd never had squid as tender and crispy as that before, and it was not served swimming in oil. The secret was in the interaction of a thin batter with fresh oil that had been heated to a high temperature and was deep-fried for a short time.

SQUID:

2 LB 3¼ OZ (1 KG) SQUID BODIES
(6–7 IN/12–15 CM LONG)
1⅔ CUPS (200 G) ALL-PURPOSE FLOUR
4 TBSP (32 G) CORNSTARCH
2 TBSP (21 G) BAKING POWDER
1⅔ CUPS (400 ML) ICE-COLD WATER
(35.6 °F/2 °C)
2 EGGS
6½ CUPS (1.5 L) PEANUT OIL

Cut up and clean the squid. Divide each mantle into three pieces. Thoroughly combine the flour, cornstarch, and baking powder. In a bowl, combine the ice-cold water with the eggs. Gradually stir in the flour mixture, and quickly beat to a smooth batter. Heat the oil to 320 °F (160 °C). Coat the squid pieces in the batter and briefly let drain, then deep-fry in the hot oil until crispy.

LIME AIOLI:

¾ CUP PLUS 1½ TBSP (200 G) JAPANESE MAYONNAISE
JUICE AND GRATED ZEST OF **1** LIME
1 TSP (5 ML) GARLIC OIL
(→ SEE BASIC RECIPES)

Combine all the ingredients and transfer to a spray bottle.

GARNISH:

FOR EACH PERSON ...
GREEN CHILI GEL (→ SEE BASIC RECIPES)
4 LETTUCE LEAVE STEMS

HAR GOW, LANGOUSTINE & BAMBOO

**Har gow is one of the most traditional dim sums in Cantonese cuisine. The wonderfully delicate dim sum pastry envelops a mixture of prawn, young bamboo and stuffing. Firm to the bite, it releases its sweetish shellfish flavors in the mouth.
In this recipe, we use luxury langoustines, also known as spiny lobsters. Please note that although these dim sum may look easy to make, they actually demand a high degree of dexterity.**

DOUGH:

4 CUPS (500 G) ALL-PURPOSE FLOUR
2 CUPS (250 G) TAPIOCA FLOUR
3 TBSP (40 ML) COLD WATER
2 TBSP (30 ML) PORK LARD
½ **CUP (125 ML)** BOILING WATER

Put the flour and the tapioca flour into a bowl and make a well in the center. Add the cold water and the lard, then add the boiling water, using two chopsticks to stir the mixture. As soon as the batter starts to thicken, start kneading the mixture vigorously with your hands. Let the dough rest for 30 minutes. Now shape the dough into longish rolls. Cut the rolls into slices the thickness of a thumb and roll each one out to a disk 3¼ in (8 cm) in diameter.
Cover each dough disk with 1½ oz (40 g) of the filling (SEE RIGHT), then close the dough over the filling. Steam the dough pockets in a bamboo steamer for 5 minutes at 180 °F (82 °C).

FILLING:

1 LB 1½ OZ (500 G) LANGOUSTINE FLESH, COOKED AND FINELY DICED
1¾ CUPS (200 G) COOKED AND FINELY DICED BAMBOO SHOOTS
7 OZ (200 G) CHICKEN STUFFING
(→ SEE BASIC RECIPES)
2 CUPS (100 G) PEELED AND FINELY DICED GINGER
½ **CUP (8 TBSP/120 ML)** LEE KUM KEE OYSTER SAUCE
6 TBSP (90 G) FINELY CHOPPED CILANTRO STEMS

In a bowl, combine all the ingredients for the filling.

GARNISH:

FOR EACH PERSON ...
3 TBSP (40 ML) SHELLFISH BROTH
(→ SEE BASIC RECIPES)

RICE WINE NOODLES, BLACK TRUFFLE & CHICKEN LUNGS

We wanted to create a dim sum with black truffles and had an idea to try it out with a pasta-like dim sum mixture. The rice wine noodles are unique in consistency: firm to the bite yet warm and tender. And the cream sauce helps the dish to become a wanderer between two culinary worlds.

RICE WINE NOODLES:

2½ CUPS (400 G) RICE FLOUR FOR BÁNH CANH RIBBON NOODLES
14 TBSP (200 ML) RICE WINE
1¼ CUPS (300 ML) DUCK BROTH
(→ SEE BASIC RECIPES)

In a bowl, combine the flour and the rice wine. Pour the mixture into a deep GN tray and steam in a Rational CombiMaster for 25 minutes at 212 °F (100 °C). Take out of the steamer and let cool. Tip the mixture onto the work surface and cut into long noodle strips. In a saucepan, bring the duck broth to a boil, add the noodles, and cook until they are firm to the bite.

TRUFFLE CREAM SAUCE:

2 CUPS PLUS 1½ TBSP (500 ML) BEEF TEA
(→ SEE BASIC RECIPES)
14 TBSP (200 ML) TRUFFLE JUICE
7 TBSP (100 ML) MARSALA
½ CUP PLUS 1 TBSP (100 G) MUSCOVADO SUGAR
2 CUPS (200 G) TRUFFLE BREAKINGS
¾ CUP PLUS 1½ TBSP (200 G) HEAVY CREAM
1¾ STICKS (¾ CUP PLUS 2 TBSP/200 G) BUTTER
1 TSP (5 ML) BONE SUCKIN' HABANERO SAUCE
CORNSTARCH

Put all the ingredients apart from the cornstarch into a sauté pan and bring to a boil. Simmer for 10 minutes, then thicken lightly with a little cornstarch.

WHITE GRAPES:

⅔ CUP (100 G) THOMPSON SEEDLESS GRAPES
3½ TBSP (50 ML) RED BULL

Vacuumize the grapes with the Red Bull and let infuse for 6 hours. Now place the grapes onto a Silpat baking mat and dehydrate in an Excalibur Dehydrator for 8 hours.

GARNISH:

FOR EACH PERSON ...
4 CHICKEN LUNGS, FRIED AND MARINATED IN A LITTLE CHEF SAUCE
2 DOTS OF RED CHILI COMPOTE
1 ESPRESSO SPOON (2.5 ML) FINELY GRATED HAZELNUT KERNELS
1 ESPRESSO SPOON (2.5 ML) HAZELNUT OIL
1½ TBSP (6 G) BLACK WINTER TRUFFLE, COOKED AND SLICED

AVOCADO, TOMATO & SHRIMP

The special feature of this dim sum is the way it is served: like Italian gnocchi. We make the dough from rice and avocado, and to stay with the same world of aromas, the dim sum gnocchi are combined with tomatoes and almonds, as well as raw shrimps.

AVOCADO DIM SUM GNOCCHI:

5 CUPS (750 G) AVOCADO FLESH
3 CUPS (750 G) COOKED JASMINE RICE
¾ CUP (180 G) EGG YOLKS
3 TBSP (45 ML) CORNSTARCH
3¼ CUPS (400 G) CHINESE WHEAT STARCH (TANG FLOUR)
½ CUP (100 G) GREEN CHILI SAUCE
(→ SEE BASIC RECIPES)
⅓ CUP (80 G) LEMON OIL
(→ SEE BASIC RECIPES)
MALDON SEA SALT

In a Thermomix, process the avocado flesh and the rice to a smooth mixture. Thoroughly stir in the egg yolks, cornstarch, and tang flour. Fold in the chili sauce and lemon oil, then season the mixture to taste with salt. Transfer the mixture into a spray bottle. Bring salted water to a boil in a large, shallow saucepan. Squirt the gnocchi mixture in long strands of ⅜ in (1 cm) diameter into the boiling water. Simmer gently for 4 minutes, then take out and let cool. Cut the strands into gnocchi. Briefly heat the avocado dim sum gnocchi in a bamboo steamer before serving.

TOMATO BROTH:

2 LB 3¼ OZ (1 KG) RIPE HONEYTOMATOES®
1 TBSP (15 ML) GROUND STAR ANISE
1 TBSP (15 ML) FINELY CHOPPED THAI RED CHILE
2 PINCHES OF GROUND CINNAMON
½ CUP PLUS 1 TBSP (100 G) DARK MUSCOVADO SUGAR

Combine all the ingredients, then puree them in three batches in a Thermomix for 1 minute each at Speed 10. Let rest for 6 hours, then strain the broth through a cheesecloth.

MARINATED TOMATOES:

20 RIPE HONEYTOMATOES®
1⅓ CUPS (300 G) PASSION FRUIT PUREE

Blanch, then skin the tomatoes. Bring the passion fruit puree to a boil and reduce to 11 tablespoons (100 g). Marinate the tomatoes in the puree, then place them on a Silpat baking mat and dehydrate in an Excalibur Dehydrator for 12 hours at 131 °F (55 °C).

ALMOND MILK GEL:

3 TBSP (40 G) ALMOND MILK
2 PINCHES OF XANTHAN GUM

Process both ingredients in a Thermomix until the mixture is creamy. Transfer the mixture to a spray bottle.

RAW SHRIMPS:

15 RAW SHRIMPS (SHELLED AND DEVEINED, HEAD AND TAIL REMOVED), CUT INTO **60** SEGMENTS
1 TBSP (15 ML) ORANGE OIL
(→ SEE BASIC RECIPES)
4 PINCHES OF PIMENT D'ESPELETTE
4 PINCHES OF MALDON SEA SALT

Marinate the prawns in the orange oil, then season with the piment d'espelette and the Maldon sea salt. Chill and serve cold.

GARNISH:

FOR EACH PERSON...
5 ALMOND SLICES, ROASTED
5 THAI BASIL LEAVES

RTR FRIED RICE

I ate the best fried rice of my life from a street vendor in Bangkok. Two sisters fried the rice in a cast-iron wok over charcoal. The "wok taste," as we call the unique flavor imparted by a particularly hot wok, and the smoky aroma from cooking over charcoal, made this bowl of fried rice simply divine. My friend, the wine merchant Jan Ganser, had taken us there, and I shall always remain grateful to him for it.

FRIED RICE:

5½ CUPS (1 KG) BASMATI RICE
CORNISH SEA SALT
VEGETABLE OIL FOR FRYING
FRESHLY GROUND WHITE PEPPER
5¼ OZ (150 G) PORK BELLY, COOKED AND FINELY DICED
5¼ OZ (150 G) NORWAY LOBSTER FLESH, COOKED AND FINELY SLICED
5¼ OZ (150 G) HONG KONG GAI LAN, CHOPPED
⅓ CUP (80 G) FINELY CHOPPED SPRING LEEK
1½ CUPS (80 G) GINGER, PEELED AND FINELY DICED
4 TBSP (60 ML) LEE KUM KEE CHILLI BEAN SAUCE
8 TBSP (120 ML) MUSHI SAUCE (→ SEE BASIC RECIPES)
8 TBSP (120 ML) LIME JUICE

Thoroughly wash the rice twice, then cook in salted water until firm to the bite. Drain and rinse in iced water. Drain again and spread out on a baking sheet to dry. Once dried, fry in a wok in a little vegetable oil until crispy. Season with Cornish sea salt and white pepper. Combine all the remaining ingredients with the rice and spread in a deep baking pan. Bake in a preheated oven for 7 minutes at 428 °F (220 °C).

SNAIL, PARSLEY & GARLIC

Snail, parsley, and garlic, the classic combination from Burgundy, is here repurposed as dim sum. At some point during my childhood — while on the hunt for culinary borderline experiences — I came across snail shells filled with snail flesh and herb butter in a low-cost supermarket's freezer chest. For years, the new-to-me peculiar texture of snails remained a highlight, especially because my classmates found them disgusting. I should have known even then what my future career was likely to be.

WONTON:

2 (7 OZ/200G) PACKAGES HAPPY BOY WONTON PASTRY

Fill the wonton squares with 1 teaspoon (5 ml) each of the filling mixture (SEE BELOW) and steam in a Rational CombiMaster for 8 minutes at 180 °F (82 °C).

FILLING:

4 TBSP (60 ML) GARLIC OIL (→ SEE BASIC RECIPES)
¼ CUP (40 G) PEELED AND FINELY DICED ONIONS
1⅓ CUPS (100 G) FINELY CHOPPED THAI WATER SPINACH
1⅓ CUPS (100 G) VERY FINELY CHOPPED CURLY PARSLEY
14 OZ (400 G) GIANT AFRICAN LAND SNAILS, INTESTINES REMOVED, STEAMED AND FINELY CHOPPED
7 OZ (200 G) CHICKEN STUFFING (→ SEE BASIC RECIPES)
5 TBSP (80 ML) MUSHI SAUCE (→ SEE BASIC RECIPES)
CORNISH SEA SALT

Heat the garlic oil in a wok, add the onions and sauté them in the oil. Add the water spinach and the parsley and fry over high heat. Transfer to a bowl and let cool.
Combine the snails, chicken stuffing, and mushi sauce and season generously with Cornish sea salt. Combine both mixtures.

GARLIC FOAM:

1¼ CUPS (300 ML) CHICKEN BROTH (→ SEE BASIC RECIPES)
¾ CUP PLUS 1½ TBSP (200 G) HEAVY CREAM
3½ TBSP (50 ML) MUSHI SAUCE
1 STICK (⅓ CUP PLUS 2 TBSP/100 G) BUTTER
CORNSTARCH
4 TBSP (60 ML) TARRAGON VINEGAR, STRAINED

In a saucepan, combine the chicken broth, cream, mushi sauce, and butter, bring to a boil and simmer for 5 minutes. Thicken with the cornstarch and flavor with the tarragon vinegar. Transfer into an iSi thermo whip, fit the bottle with two cream chargers, and keep warm. Shake vigorously before using.

GARNISH:

FOR EACH PERSON ....
1 TBSP (15 ML) PARSLEY DRESSING (→ SEE BASIC RECIPES)
5 STEMS OF PERSINETTE® CRESS
5 GARLIC CHIPS (→ SEE BASIC RECIPES)
1 TSP (5 ML) SWEET AND SOUR RED ONIONS (→ SEE BASIC RECIPES)

JAPANESE TUNA PIZZA

We invented this Japanese tuna pizza after hearing about Wolfgang Puck's legendary salmon pizza in LA. This dish brings together a variety of temperatures and textures, at the same time appealing to many people as everyone is familiar with pizza. In fact, authentic pizza dough did not really go well with a topping of tuna sashimi and crunchy yellow radish. With a little luck, and even more happenstance, I came across the Indian roti prata dough, which is fried at a high heat and turns out wonderfully crispy. Thus was born a dish which we serve not only as dim sum at Restaurant Tim Raue, but which also quickly advanced to the dish of choice with diners at my Hanami by Tim Raue casual Asian dining restaurant on the *Mein Schiff 5* cruise ship.

DIM SUM DOUGH:

10 DISKS OF ROTI PRATA DOUGH, **4 IN (10 CM)** DIAMETER
VEGETABLE OIL

In a frying pan, fry each dough disk in 2 tablespoons (30 ml) of oil on both sides until crispy.

TOPPING:

2 LB 3¼ OZ (1 KG) TUNA FILLET, SASHIMI QUALITY
7 TBSP (100 ML) HOT BANANA KETCHUP
5 TBSP (80 ML) MUSHI SAUCE (→ SEE BASIC RECIPES)
8 TBSP (120 ML) FINELY CHOPPED CILANTRO STEMS
6 TBSP (90 ML) PEELED AND FINELY DICED GINGER

Cut the fish into ½ in (1 cm) dice. Stir together the remaining ingredients and marinate the tuna in the mixture. Divide the mixture between ten circular cookie cutters 3¼ in (8 cm) in diameter.

GARNISH:

FOR EACH PERSON …
8 SMALL CUBES OF JAPANESE YELLOW RADISH
2 PINCHES OF WASABI SESAME SEEDS
2 PINCHES OF PIMENT D'ESPELETTE
8 STEMS OF CILANTRO CRESS

fish

How do you define fresh fish?

In Chinese cuisine, especially in Shanghai, it is customary to choose a live fish from a water tank, which is then instantly killed and prepared, and will be on the table only a few minutes later. In Germany this is what happens with trout and char.

Every day the Chinatown Wet Market in Singapore sells fish caught only a few hours earlier, regional fish that are swimming in water tanks and prepared à la minute for the customer.

That is truly fresh fish.

The main characteristic of freshness is a swim bladder that is still full to bursting. To demonstrate freshness, the fish are halved and presented in such a way that the swim bladder virtually jumps out at the potential buyer. There are also exotics for sale at the Wet Market, including frogs, crocodile meat, and sea turtles.

The latter in particular are endangered and as such protected in many countries, but unfortunately some consumers are not at all interested in animal conservation.

Whenever you come across live turtles for sale, you had better desist.

ZANDER, KAMEBISHI SOY BROTH, LEEK & GINGER

Together with Wasabi Langoustine and Peking Duck, this dish is one of the three best I've ever created. Based on whole steamed fish with leek and ginger in soy sauce — a dish that is widely cooked in China — this recipe is an example of my approach to, and my interpretation of, the Chinese classics.
With hot water and dry ice we simulate steaming the fish in a bamboo basket at the table. The ingredients are the same, but they are presented in a more elegant and delicate fashion — the fish is filleted, without tiresome skin, scales, and bones. It's served with leek in a variety of textures, to create a more complex aromatic presence, and soy stock in the form of a multi-layered broth. And, instead of plain oil, we use a subtle, clarified butter as part of the garnish.

ZANDER:

10 ZANDER FILLETS, ABOUT **3 OZ (80 G)** EACH, WEIGHING AT LEAST **9 LB (4 KG)** IN TOTAL, SKIN AND BONES REMOVED
LEMON OIL (→ SEE BASIC RECIPES)

Marinate the zander fillets in lemon oil. Place them on a baking sheet and steam in a Rational CombiMaster for 7 minutes at 180 °F (82 °C). Then put them into a Lohberger Cook'n'Hold for 10 minutes at 156 °F (69 °C).

KAMEBISHI SOY BROTH:

2 LB 3¼ OZ (1 KG) DUCK LEG
3½ TBSP (50 ML) KAMEBISHI SOY SAUCE, MATURED IN A WOODEN BARREL FOR 10 YEARS
14 TBSP (200 ML) ROSE'S LEMON CORDIAL
7 TBSP (100 ML) MUSHI SAUCE (→ SEE BASIC RECIPES)
3½ TBSP (50 ML) YUZU JUICE
⅔ CUP (60 G) THIN SLICES PEELED GINGER
1 GREEN THAI CHILE, FINELY CHOPPED
¾ CUP PLUS 1 TSP (150 G) MUSCOVADO SUGAR
2 TBSP (60 ML) TABASCO GREEN PEPPER SAUCE
1 CUP (100 G) FINELY CHOPPED CELERY
1 CUP PLUS 2 TBSP (100 G) FINELY CHOPPED LEEKS
3 QUARTS PLUS ¾ CUP (3 L) WATER
2 CUPS PLUS 2 TBSP (500 ML) EGG WHITE

Put all the ingredients apart from the egg white into a saucepan and bring to a boil. Simmer for 90 minutes. Strain the broth through a cheesecloth and let cool. Stir in the egg white, gently bring the broth back to a boil, and slowly fish out the set egg white to leave behind a clear broth. Strain through a cheesecloth.

GARNISH:

FOR EACH PERSON …
5 DOTS OF LEEK AND GINGER PUREE (→ SEE BASIC RECIPES)
4 SLICES OF YOUNG GINGER (→ SEE BASIC RECIPES)
1 TBSP (15 ML) CLARIFIED BUTTER
5 PIECES OF SPRING LEEK, SAUTÉED IN A WOK
1 ESPRESSO SPOON (2.5 ML) SPRING LEEK, CUT INTO PAPER-THIN STRIPS AND STORED IN ICED WATER

HAMACHI, COLOCASIA & JADE

The sauce in this dish is named for the color of the precious gemstone jade, which is highly esteemed in China as the symbol of immortality. It combines a variety of different green vegetables and chiles. As it is served cold, it is particularly suitable for warm spring or summer days. Jade sauce has a rather bitter flavor for Western tastebuds, as it contains hardly any sweetness from fruits.

HAMACHI:

8 CUPS (2 L) VEGETABLE OIL
10 SLICES OF HAMACHI FILLET
(3 OZ/80 G EACH)
CORNISH SEA SALT
GREEN CHILI GEL (→ SEE BASIC RECIPES)

Heat the oil to exactly 158 °F (70 °C), add the fish fillets and cook for 12 minutes. Take out and drain on paper towels. Season the fish with Cornish sea salt and green chili gel.

JADE SAUCE:

1 BULB FENNEL
1 BUNCH CELERY
1 HEAD LETTUCE
6⅔ CUPS (200 G) SPINACH
1 GREEN APPLE
1 LARGE SHALLOT, FINELY DICED
1 CUP (30 G) TARRAGON
7 TBSP (100 ML) ROSE'S LEMON CORDIAL
3½ TBSP (50 ML) TARRAGON VINEGAR
1 TBSP PLUS 1 TSP (20 ML) MARINADE FROM A JAR OF PICKLED JALAPEÑO PEPPERS
5 TBSP (80 ML) GREEN CHILI SAUCE (→ SEE BASIC RECIPES)

Extract the juice from the fennel, celery, lettuce, spinach, and apple. Put the juices with the remaining ingredients into a saucepan and bring to a boil. Let cool, then strain through a fine-mesh strainer.

GARNISH:

FOR EACH PERSON ...
2 SLICES OF COLOCASIA (TARO, DASHEEN, EDDOE)
2 NONPAREILLES CAPERS
2 SANSHO BERRIES
2 BALLS OF GALIA MELON
½ WHITE PEARL ONION (→ SEE BASIC RECIPES)
1 DILL FROND
1 ESPRESSO SPOON (2.5 ML) LEMON VERBENA OIL
3 DOTS OF WHITE ONION CREAM (→ SEE BASIC RECIPES)

SEA BASS, PARSLEY & ALBA TRUFFLE

Sea bass with Alba truffles, Thai water spinach, and hazelnut is a classic in my kitchen, and the recipe below represents an elegant variation. The dish is now altogether lighter and subtler than previous versions, and is indicative of the new direction that my cooking is taking.

SEA BASS:

10 SEA BASS FILLETS, **3½ OZ (100 G)** EACH, FROM FISH WEIGHING AT LEAST **11 LB 1½ OZ (5 KG)**, SKIN AND BONES REMOVED
CLARIFIED BUTTER
CORNISH SEA SALT
GREEN CHILI GEL (→ SEE BASIC RECIPES)

Marinate the sea bass fillets in the clarified butter. Place on a baking sheet and cover with plastic wrap. Steam in a Rational CombiMaster for 5 minutes at 180 °F (82 °C), then place in a Lohberger Cook'n'Hold for 10 minutes at 156 °F (69 °C). Season the fillets with salt and dress with the chili gel.

PARSLEY ROOT FOAM:

4 CUPS (400 G) PARSLEY ROOTS, CUT INTO THIN SLICES
⅔ CUP (100 G) PEELED AND VERY FINELY DICED WHITE ONIONS
3½ TBSP (50 G) BUTTER
4½ CUPS (1 L) CHICKEN BROTH (→ SEE BASIC RECIPES)
2½ CUPS (600 ML) WATER
2 CUPS (500 ML) MILK
1 CUP (250 G) HEAVY CREAM
10 TBSP (150 ML) ROSE'S LEMON CORDIAL
CORNSTARCH

Put the parsley roots and the onions into a large saucepan and sauté in the butter without browning. Add all the liquids and simmer everything for 30 minutes. Puree with a hand blender until smooth. Bring to a boil, then strain through a fine-mesh strainer.
Return to a boil, then thicken with a little cornstarch until it is syrupy. Strain through a fine-mesh strainer and transfer to an iSi soda siphon. Fit the siphon with two cream chargers and keep warm. Shake well before use.

PARSLEY ROOTS:

20 SLICES OF PARSLEY ROOTS, HALVED LENGTHWAYS AND BLANCHED
JUICE OF **2** LIMES
FRESHLY GROUND WHITE PEPPER

Vacuumize the parsley root slices together with the lime juice. Let infuse for 2 minutes, then take out again. Roll up the parsley root slices and season generously with white pepper.

GARNISH:

FOR EACH PERSON …
6 STEMS PERSINETTE® CRESS
2 TSP (3 G) ALBA TRUFFLES, SHAVED INTO SLICES
6 DOTS OF PARSLEY ROOT CREAM (→ SEE BASIC RECIPES)

SOM TAM-O & SALMON HEAD

In Phuket I ate som tam-o for the first time and was deeply impressed. Chef Kla, the head of cuisine at the Trisara Resort, invited me into his kitchen and showed me how it was prepared. The specific challenge is the ratio of the ingredients to one another. In my restaurant too, every som tam-o tastes different from the next. This is what makes it particularly exciting!

SOM TAM-O:

THE FLESH OF **2** POMELOS
3 GREEN APPLES, FINELY DICED
2 LETTUCE HEARTS, CUT INTO FINE STRIPS
4 TBSP (60 ML) KONINGSVOGEL SAMBAL MANIS
4 TBSP (40 G) FRIED ONIONS
4 TBSP (20 G) VERY FINELY DICED RED THAI SHALLOTS
4 TBSP (12 G) PEELED AND VERY FINELY DICED GINGER
4 TBSP (12 G) VERY FINELY CHOPPED LEMONGRASS
6 TBSP (25 G) MACADAMIA NUTS, ROASTED AND ROUGHLY CRUSHED
4 TBSP (60 ML) LIME JUICE
4 TBSP (60 ML) VEGETABLE OIL

Combine all the ingredients in a bowl.

SALMON HEAD:

10 SALMON HEADS
5 QUARTS PLUS 1¼ CUPS (5 L) VEGETABLE OIL

Place the salmon heads into deep GN trays. Heat the vegetable oil to 176 °F (80 °C), pour it into the trays and cook the salmon heads in the oven for 30 minutes at 140 °F (60 °C). Carefully remove the heads from the trays and, using a gourmet spoon, remove the cheeks, the fatty skin on the bridge of the nose, and the chin.

GREEN APPLE FOAM:

14 TBSP (200 ML) GREEN APPLE JUICE
7 TBSP (100 G) HEAVY CREAM
3½ TBSP (50 ML) GREEN CHILI SAUCE, STRAINED (→ SEE BASIC RECIPES)

Stir all the ingredients together, transfer to an iSi soda siphon, and fit the siphon with two cream chargers.

GARNISH:

FOR EACH PERSON ...
1 ESPRESSO SPOON (2.5 ML) VERY THIN STRIPS OF LEMON LEAF

TURBOT, PEAS & MELON

This dish is fantastically rich in contrasts: velvety pea puree, sweet melon, salty dashi, and salty bonito flakes, all combined with a rich piece of turbot, one of the finest of all sea fish. It is not very spicy and altogether quite Japanese in character. I like it very much because it radiates an incredible warmth and passion, being wonderfully full-flavored at the same time.

TURBOT:

10 TURBOT FILETS, **3 OZ (80 G)** EACH,
OF FISH WEIGHING AT LEAST **13 LB (6 KG)**
CLARIFIED BUTTER
½ **CUP (5 G)** EXTRA FINE BONITO FLAKES

In a skillet or frying pan, fry the turbot fillets in clarified butter on one side, one at a time. Place them onto baking sheets, cover with plastic wrap, and steam in a Rational CombiMaster for 4 minutes at 180 °F (82 °C). Remove the wrap and put the baking sheets into a Lohberger Cook'n'Hold for 10 minutes at 156 °F (69 °C). Dress the turbot fillets with the dashi jelly (SEE BELOW) and sprinkle with bonito flakes.

DASHI JELLY:

1⅔ CUPS (400 ML) DASHI
(→ SEE BASIC RECIPES)
10 TBSP (150 ML) ROSE'S LEMON CORDIAL
2 TBSP (8 G) AGAR AGAR POWDER

In a saucepan, bring the dashi and the lemon cordial to a boil. Stir in the agar agar powder and simmer for 5 minutes. Pour the mixture onto a baking pan and let cool. Transfer to a Thermomix and process to a smooth mixture. Transfer to a spray bottle.

PEA PUREE:

4½ STICKS (2 CUPS PLUS 3½ TBSP/ 500 G) BUTTER
5 WHITE ONIONS, PEELED AND FINELY DICED
4 GREEN THAI CHILES
2 LB 3¼ OZ (1 KG) FRESH GARDEN PEAS, HULLED
CORNISH SEA SALT
8 CUPS (2 L) MILK
10½ OZ (300 G) SUGAR
4½ CUPS (1 L) WATER

Heat the butter in a saucepan. Add the onions and the chiles and sauté in the butter, then add the peas. Season generously with Cornish sea salt. Add the milk, sugar, and water and bring to a boil. Simmer until the peas are very soft. In a Thermomix, process everything on Speed 10 to a smooth puree.

MELON BALLS:

¼ GALIA MELON
4 TBSP (60 ML) RICE VINEGAR
2 TBSP (30 ML) ROSE'S LEMON CORDIAL
XANTHAN GUM

Using a small melon baller, cut out 60 balls from the melon. In a Thermomix, puree the remaining melon flesh together with the rice vinegar and the lemon cordial. Thicken with a little xanthan to a syrupy consistency. Place the melon balls into the liquid.

GARNISH:

FOR EACH PERSON …
2 DOTS OF GINGER JELLY
(→ SEE BASIC RECIPES)
1 TBSP (6 G) FRESHLY HULLED PEAS
6 STEMS OF ACLLA CRESS®
3 SQUARES OF GINGER, **¼ × ¼ IN (5 × 5 MM)**

RASCASSE, FISH MAW & HEARTLEAF ICEPLANT

The scorpion fish, or rascasse as it is known in French, is my absolute favorite among fish. With my best friend Till, I visited a market in southern France and bought a splendid 6½-lb (3-kg) specimen. The mighty head with its giant mouth and impressive teeth seemed rather threatening. The firm, snow-white flesh has a superb texture and an overwhelmingly meaty aroma; unfortunately, the yield is rather small. And it is a real struggle to fillet the scorpion fish. It is an utterly uneconomic fish, one that goes well with the ultra-expensive fish maw, the fish's swim bladder.

RASCASSE:

10 SCORPION FISH FILLETS, OF FISH WEIGHING **2LB 3¼ OZ–4½ LB (1–2 KG)**
VEGETABLE OIL
3½ TBSP (50 ML) YUZU JUICE
CORNISH SEA SALT
20 SANSHO BERRIES

Cook the fillets for 15 minutes in the oil heated to 162 °F (72 °C). Take out, pat dry, and season with the yuzu juice and the Cornish sea salt. Place 2 sansho berries on top of each fillet.

FISH MAW BROTH:

1 FISH MAW. WEIGHING **1 LB 1½ OZ (500 G)**
2 LB 3¼ OZ (1 KG) CHICKEN LEGS
2 LB 3¼ OZ (1 KG) VEAL, DICED
2 CUPS PLUS 1½ TBSP (500 ML) ROSE'S LEMON CORDIAL
1¼ CUPS (300 ML) GREEN CHILI SAUCE (→ SEE BASIC RECIPES)
1¼ CUPS (300 ML) ELDERFLOWER SYRUP
3 CUPS (1 KG 125 G) OF FINELY CHOPPED SPRING LEEKS
⅔ CUP (30 G) PEELED AND FINELY CHOPPED GINGER
1 LB 1½ OZ (500 G) GROUND VEAL
1¼ CUPS (300 ML) EGG WHITE
CORNISH SEA SALT
3 RAMIRO POINTED PEPPERS
LEMON OIL (→ SEE BASIC RECIPES)
2 TSP (10 ML) GRATED YUZU ZEST

Bring 3 quarts plus ¾ cup (3 l) water to a boil, add the fish maw, and cover the saucepan with a lid. Let infuse for 6 hours. Repeat the process. Take out the fish maw and cut into ⅜ in (1 cm) dice.
To make the broth, put all the ingredients apart from the ground veal, egg white, salt, peppers, lemon oil, and yuzu zest into a large saucepan together with 4 quarts plus ¾ cup (4 l) water, bring to a boil, then simmer for 2 hours. The broth should be reduced to 6½ cups (1.5 l). Strain the broth and let cool completely. Now stir the ground veal and the egg white together and add to the cold broth. Slowly bring to a boil, then simmer for 15 minutes. Strain the broth through a cheesecloth and season with Cornish sea salt.
Halve and deseed the peppers, then cut the flesh into diamonds. Fry in a wok, in a little lemon oil.
Add the broth, peppers and fish maw dice to a sauté pan and bring to a boil. Add the yuzu zest.

CORDIFOLIA GEL:

7 TBSP (100 ML) ELDERFLOWER SYRUP
7 TBSP (100 ML) GILOY (TINOSPORA CORDIFOLIA) JUICE
1 TBSP (4 G) AGAR AGAR POWDER

In a saucepan, bring the syrup and the giloy juice to a boil with 10 tablespoons (150 ml) water. Stir in the agar agar powder and simmer for 5 minutes. Pour the liquid into a baking pan and let cool. In a Thermomix, process everything to a smooth mixture and transfer to a spray bottle.

GARNISH:

FOR EACH PERSON …
3 HEARTLEAF ICEPLANT LEAVES

JOHN DORY NO. 219

I wanted to include a Chinese wok recipe with fish in my repertoire, and to satirize Chinese menus we gave the John Dory a number in the title, instead of naming the ingredients as is normally done. The number stands for two stars in the *Michelin* Guide and nineteen points in the *Gault Millau* Guide.

JOHN DORY:

6 JOHN DORY FILLETS, FROM FISH WEIGHING **4½ LB (2 KG)**, SKIN REMOVED
1½ CUPS (200 G) CORNSTARCH
FAT FOR DEEP-FRYING

Cut the fillets into ¾ in (2 cm) pieces. Dip the fillet pieces into the cornstarch and coat with it. Let rest for 1 hour, then deep-fry in a wok in fat heated to 374 °F (190 °C). Take out and immediately place in a sauté pan with the tamarind sauce (SEE RIGHT) to glaze. Be careful, the dish is extremely hot!

TAMARIND SAUCE:

2 CUPS PLUS 1½ TBSP (500 ML) BEEF TEA (→ SEE BASIC RECIPES)
1½ CUPS (400 G) SEEDLESS TAMARIND PASTE
1¼ CUPS (300 ML) SUREE PHAT THAI SAUCE
1½ CUPS (200 G) PALM SUGAR
7 TBSP (100 ML) ROSE'S LEMON CORDIAL
3 TBSP (45 ML) BONE SUCKIN' HABANERO SAUCE
2 TBSP (20 G) CORNISH SEA SALT
CORNSTARCH

Bring all the ingredients apart from the cornstarch to a boil in a sauté pan, then lightly thicken with a little cornstarch.

GARNISH:

FOR EACH PERSON ...
2 TBSP (15 G) COARSELY CHOPPED CASHEWS
1 TBSP (15 ML) YOUNG GINGER (→ SEE BASIC RECIPES)
2 HONG KONG GAI LAN, BLANCHED

MACKEREL, SHISO, PONZU & JERUSALEM ARTICHOKE

When we were invited to cook at the Busan Seafood Festival in South Korea, the organizers requested we cook a mackerel course. Since Busan boasts culinary influences from Japan, we created a dish comprising German Jerusalem artichokes, which we had specially flown in, Japanese ponzu and shiso, and Korean mackerel. We served our dish outdoors, in front of the Maritime Museum of Busan, to 350 guests — and were rewarded with an almighty round of applause.

MACKEREL:

10 MACKERELS
10 TBSP (100 G) CORNISH SEA SALT
½ **CUP (100 G)** SUGAR

Fillet the mackerel, cut away the bones and the belly flaps. Place the fillets onto a baking sheet. Combine the salt and the sugar and sprinkle over the fillets. Let stand for 15 minutes, then rinse the fillets and pat them dry. Place onto a baking sheet and cold-smoke twice in a smoking oven. Cut the fillets as sashimi and cook briefly under a salamander.

PONZU BROTH:

2 TBSP (30 ML) KAMEBISHI SOY SAUCE, MATURED IN A WOODEN BARREL FOR 5 YEARS
2 TBSP (30 ML) MIRIN
3½ TBSP (50 ML) RICE VINEGAR
3½ TBSP (50 ML) MANDARIN JUICE
3½ TBSP (50 ML) YUZU JUICE
7 TBSP (100 ML) BEEF TEA
(→ SEE BASIC RECIPES)
2 SHISO LEAVES
½ GREEN THAI CHILE

Combine all the ingredients and puree in a Thermomix for 1 minute on Speed 10.

GARNISH:

FOR EACH PERSON ...
5 PIECES OF DEEP-FRIED JERUSALEM ARTICHOKE PEEL
4 ROUND **SLICES** OF SHISO LEAVES
3 SLICES OF RAW JERUSALEM ARTICHOKES
7 DOTS OF JERUSALEM ARTICHOKE PUREE
(→ SEE BASIC RECIPES)

COD, WASABI & CRESS

Every day, we receive supplies of fresh cod from Norway. It is as white as snow, and if you eat it raw, you can taste the ice-cold, slightly salty water in which it lived. It doesn't smell one little bit of fish, only of pure ocean. The ingredients all around the fish in this dish are structured like a Japanese garden, enhancing it with green, strong, radish, and herbal aromas.

COD:

10 COD FILLETS, **3¼ OZ (90 G)** EACH
4 TBSP (60 ML) LEMON OIL
(→ SEE BASIC RECIPES)
CORNISH SEA SALT

Marinate the cod in the lemon oil. Steam the fish in a Rational CombiMaster for 5 minutes at 180 °F (82 °C), then put it into a Lohberger Cook'n'Hold for 15 minutes at 156 °F (69 °C). Season with Cornish sea salt.

WASABI BEURRE BLANC:

14 TBSP (200 ML) CHICKEN BROTH
(→ SEE BASIC RECIPES)
7 TBSP (100 G) HEAVY CREAM
6 TBSP (⅓ **CUP/80 G**) BUTTER
CORNSTARCH
1 TBSP (15 ML) NISHIKIDÔRI MARKET WASABI PASTE
CORNISH SEA SALT

In a sauté pan, bring the chicken broth to a boil with the cream and the butter. Lightly thicken the stock with cornflour, then flavor with wasabi and salt.

RADISH:

30 SLICES OF WHITE RADISH, **⅜ IN (1 CM)** THICK
4 TBSP (60 ML) RICE VINEGAR
4 TBSP (60 ML) ROSE'S LEMON CORDIAL

Using a round cutter, cut 1¼ in (3 cm) disks from the radish slices. Put the radish into a vacuum bag together with the rice vinegar and the lemon cordial and vacuumize. Let everything infuse for 3 hours.

GARDEN CRESS CREAM:

12 CUPS (600 G) GARDEN CRESS
14 OZ (400 G) PARSLEY ROOT PUREE
(→ SEE BASIC RECIPES)

Cut off the upper parts of the garden cress. Briefly blanch the cuttings in salted water, transfer to a Pacojet beaker, and freeze. Pacotize and level the mixture, then freeze again for 3 hours and pacotize again. Repeat this process four times, until the mixture has become a powder. Work the cress powder into the parsley root puree.

GARNISH:

FOR EACH PERSON …
6 HALVED PEARL ONIONS
3 SMALL **BOUQUETS** OF GARDEN CRESS

LONGBEACH
CREATOR OF THE ORIGINAL AND THE BEST BLACK PEPPER CRAB OF SINGAPORE
深海游水红斑
Live Deep Sea Red Grouper
请勿把手伸入鱼池内
Please refrain from putting your hand into the fish tank
阿拉斯加北极贝
Alaskan Hokkigai (Surf Clams)

crustaceans and seafood

In my youth, luxury meant shrimp, especially North Sea shrimp, but I also learned to rate lobster as absolute luxuries from an early age. But both became no more than minor players once I'd enjoyed my first langoustine. My admiration for these wonderfully juicy, slightly sweet, delicately aromatic creatures is immense.

And so I am all the more thrilled that in the last few years Wasabi Langoustine has replaced Peking Duck as my signature dish.

In Singapore, I was served abalone and fish maw for the first time. I soon had to realize, though, that these singular ingredients do not enthuse diners in Europe nearly as much as in Asia, and that their high price causes consternation rather than appreciation.

The paradise for all these foods is based in the East Coast Seafood Centre in Singapore. In its restaurants there is an entire aquarium wall full of live shrimp, giant red king crab, and serrated swimming crab from Sri Lanka, which are used to make chili crab, the Singaporean national dish, as well as the curious Pacific geoduck, precious abalone, and cobble stone-sized oysters. The live creatures are prepared à la minute — so fresh we can only dream about it in Europe.

WASABI LANGOUSTINE

This dish sums me up like no other. If I had to reduce my entire career to a single dish, then it would have to be Wasabi Langoustine. This plate has it all, different textures, such as crispy, delicate, and crunchy; hot and cold; sour and sweet; salty and spicy; creamy and runny. A roller coaster on the palate. This plate is me.

The original dish, known as wasabi shrimp, consists of shrimp coated in cornstarch and deep-fried. The garnish is a wasabi mayonnaise and a few slices of fresh fruits. In 2004, it was *the* trending dish in Hong Kong and Singapore. The special feature by Chinese standards is the addition of the Japanese ingredient wasabi. For them, it's roughly the same as if we had the Germans and the Dutch playing in one national soccer team.

LANGOUSTINE:

10 LANGOUSTINE TAILS, CALIBRATION 3/5
7 TBSP (100 ML) GOGI TEMPURA FLOUR, STIRRED INTO WATER
FAT FOR DEEP-FRYING

Devein the langoustine tails, wash, and pat dry. Pull through the tempura flour batter, then deep-fry for 4 minutes in fat heated to 365 °F (185 °C).

GREEN RICE FLAKES:

¼ CUP (30 G) GREEN RICE FLAKES
FAT FOR DEEP-FRYING
CORNISH SEA SALT

Deep-fry the rice flakes for a few seconds in fat heated to 365 °F (185 °C). Place onto paper towels, pat dry, and season immediately with Cornish sea salt.

MANGO GEL:

10 TBSP (150 ML) NAM DOK MAI MANGO PUREE
10 TBSP (150 ML) PASSION FRUIT PUREE
¾ TBSP (3 G) AGAR AGAR POWDER

Bring the two purees to a boil, stir in the agar agar powder, and simmer for 3 minutes. Transfer the mixture to a Thermomix bowl and let cool, then process to a smooth gel. Transfer to a spray bottle.

VINAIGRETTE:

14 TBSP (200 ML) MUSHI SAUCE, STRAINED (→ SEE BASIC RECIPES)
10 TBSP (150 ML) ROSE'S LEMON CORDIAL
10 TBSP (150 ML) RICE VINEGAR
3½ TBSP (50 ML) LIME JUICE
XANTHAN GUM
1 CUP (150 G) PEELED AND FINELY DICED CARROTS
1 CUP (150 G) PEELED AND FINELY DICED UNRIPE THAI MANGO
1½ CUPS (70 G) PEELED AND FINELY DICED GINGER
2 TBSP (15 G) FINELY CHOPPED CILANTRO STEMS

Combine all the liquid ingredients and thicken lightly with xanthan. Now stir all the remaining ingredients into the vinaigrette.

GARNISH:

FOR EACH PERSON ...
4 STEMS GHOA CRESS®
2 TBSP (30 ML) WASABI MAYONNAISE
(→ SEE BASIC RECIPES)

KING CRAB & MISO SOUP

Miso soup is the national dish of Japan. There, you eat it after the sushi rather than before, as we tend to do in the West. When combined with the wonderfully tender flesh of king crabs it results in a comforting, warming meal. But beware the Thai yellow chiles — they are very spicy indeed!

MISO SOUP:

1 GALLON PLUS ¾ CUP (4 L) EVIAN WATER
3 CUPS PLUS 3 TBSP (750 ML) ROSE'S LEMON CORDIAL
2 LB 3¼ OZ (1 KG) CHICKEN LEGS
¾ CUP (200 G) WHITE MISO PASTE
10 CUPS (100 G) BONITO FLAKES
1⅔ CUPS (250 G) PEELED AND FINELY DICED CELERY ROOT
1⅔ CUPS (250 G) PEELED AND FINELY DICED WHITE ONIONS
1 CUP PLUS 2 TBSP (250 G) FINELY DICED LEEKS
2½ CUPS (250 G) FINELY DICED CELERY
⅔ CUP (50 G) WAKAME SEAWEED
½ CUP (50 G) WHITE PEPPERCORNS, DEEP-FRIED FOR **1** MINUTE IN VEGETABLE OIL
PARED **ZESTS** OF **2** LEMONS

Put all the ingredients together into a saucepan and bring to a boil. Simmer the soup for 1 hour, then pass it through a chinois strainer.

RED KING CRAB:

10 RED KING CRAB LEGS
LEMON OIL FOR FRYING
(→ SEE BASIC RECIPES)

Cut the leg shells open lengthwise and separate out the flesh. In a skillet or frying pan, fry the flesh in the lemon oil on both sides without browning. Cover with a lid, take the pan off the heat, and let the flesh infuse.

GARNISH:

FOR EACH PERSON ...
1 STEM OF A SHIMEJI MUSHROOM
3 STRIPS OF MOROCCAN PRESERVED LEMON ZESTS
1 TSP (4 G) RED AND GREEN JAPANESE SEAWEED
1 ESPRESSO SPOON (2.5 ML) LEMON OIL
(→ SEE BASIC RECIPES)
2 SLICES OF THAI YELLOW CHILE
4 SLICES OF YOUNG GINGER
(→ SEE BASIC RECIPES)
1 PIECE OF SILKEN TOFU, CUT INTO A STAR SHAPE
1 TBSP BALLS OF YELLOW RADISH, PRESERVED IN RICE WINE

ABALONE, GINGER BEER SAUCE & GREEN RADISH

I ate my first abalone in a grill restaurant in Tokyo. The live "sea ear" was cooked whole on a teppanyaki grill, in front of the guests' eyes. The abalone is a type of snail of which you eat the foot muscle; and it can be rather a tough affair if you don't cook it the right way. I racked up a few unsuccessful attempts until Roland Trettl, then the director of cuisine at the Hangar-7 in Salzburg, gave me a good tip: He told me to use a pressure cooker.

If you are going to make the effort of preparing abalones, you should be keen on the special textures of the foods used in Chinese and Japanese cuisine. Quite apart from their stellar price, it's worth knowing that abalones have next to no aroma of their own. In order not to overpower them, we serve them with only the merest hint of a sauce.

ABALONE:

10 FRESH ABALONE, **7 OZ (200 G)** EACH
CORNISH SEA SALT
A HANDFUL OF WAKAME SEAWEED

Separate the abalones from their shells and devein. Cook with a handful of wakame seaweed in salted water in a pressure cooker for 25 minutes on setting 1.

GINGER BEER SAUCE:

4½ CUPS (1 L) CHICKEN BROTH
(→ SEE BASIC RECIPES)
1⅔ CUPS (400 ML) GINGER BEER
7 TBSP (100 ML) ROSE'S LEMON CORDIAL
2 TBSP (30 ML) TABASCO GREEN PEPPER SAUCE

Put all the ingredients into a sauté pan and boil until reduced by one-third. Just before serving, foam up the sauce with a hand blender.

GARNISH:

FOR EACH PERSON ...
3 SLICES OF GREEN RADISH, CUT INTO A MAPLE LEAF SHAPE
3 SLICES OF THOMPSON GRAPES
NORI SEAWEED JULIENNE

FISH MAW, SANSHO & HEARTLEAF ICEPLANT

Fish maw is the dried swim bladder of large fish — and one of the most expensive foods in the world. Only about fifteen years ago, 2 pounds (1 kilogram) of dried fish maw of a medium quality cost just under 30 dollars, but today the same product will set you back 600 dollars, and the trend is rising. Why is that? The Chinese eat fish maw because they believe that eating this organ, which keeps the fish in balance, will help them achieve an inner balance. And as increasing numbers of Chinese people become wealthy, they are able to afford such luxuries.

The swim bladder is a very clean organ with a gelatinous texture but without flavor. It is therefore important to serve it with an intensely aromatic sauce. It's best not to use the swim bladders of fresh fish in the kitchen.

FISH MAW:

1 FISH MAW (**1LB 1½ OZ/500 G**)
3 QUARTS PLUS ¾ CUP (3 L) WATER

Bring the water to a boil, add the fish maw, and cover the saucepan with a lid. Let stand for 6 hours, then repeat the process. Cut the fish maw into 1¼ in (3 cm) pieces.

BROTH:

2 LB 3¼ OZ (1 KG) CHICKEN LEGS
2 LB 3¼ OZ (1 KG) VEAL, DICED
2 CUPS PLUS 1½ TBSP (500 ML) ROSE'S LEMON CORDIAL
1¼ CUPS (300 ML) GREEN CHILI SAUCE (→ SEE BASIC RECIPES)
1¼ CUPS (300 ML) ELDERFLOWER SYRUP
5 CUPS (1 KG 125 G) OF SPRING LEEKS, FINELY CHOPPED
½ CUP (30 G) PEELED AND FINELY CHOPPED GINGER
1 GALLON ¾ CUP (4 L) WATER
1 LB 1 ¼ OZ (500 G) GROUND VEAL
1¼ CUPS (300 ML) EGG WHITE
CORNISH SEA SALT

In a large saucepan, combine all the ingredients apart from the ground veal, egg white, and salt. Bring to a boil, then simmer for 2 hours. The broth should be reduced to 6½ cups (1.5 l) after cooking. Strain the broth and let cool.
Stir together the ground veal and the egg white, then add the cold broth. Slowly bring to a boil and simmer for 15 minutes. Strain the broth through a cheesecloth and season with Cornish sea salt.

RAMIRO PEPPERS:

10 RAMIRO POINTED PEPPERS
LEMON OIL (→ SEE BASIC RECIPES)

Halve the peppers, remove the seeds, then cut the flesh into diamond shapes. Fry the pieces in a wok in little lemon oil until soft.

GARNISH:

FOR EACH PERSON ...
4 NISHIKIDÔRI MARKET PRESERVED SANSHO BERRIES
1 TSP (5 ML) LEMON OIL (→ SEE BASIC RECIPES)
1 TSP (5 ML) FINELY GRATED YUZU ZEST
4 HEARTLEAF ICEPLANT LEAVES

HONG KONG GAI LAN, OYSTER SAUCE & LIME

There are a few vegetable dishes in Cantonese cuisine that are very easy to prepare yet utterly delicious. My favorite is Hong Kong gai lan and oyster sauce. This dish is composed of Hong Kong gai lan, a small-growing broccoli, and a translucent, ready-made, bottled sauce, which consists of dried oysters, water, and a little ginger. For our own version, we brought the oysters to the foreground, and arranged the gai lan and the ginger around them.

OYSTERS:

10 GILLARDEAU OYSTERS,
3½ OZ (**100 G**) EACH

Open the oysters, place them on a baking sheet covered with baking paper, and cook in a Rational CombiMaster for 90 seconds at 180 °F (82 °C).

OYSTER SAUCE:

8 GILLARDEAU OYSTERS, **3½ OZ** (**100 G**) EACH
3 TBSP (**40 ML**) AGAVE NECTAR
2 CUPS PLUS 1½ TBSP (**500 ML**) BEEF TEA
(→ SEE BASIC RECIPES)
1¾ CUPS PLUS 2 TBSP (**450 ML**) DASHI
(→ SEE BASIC RECIPES)
3 TBSP (**50 ML**) CHEF SAUCE
(→ SEE BASIC RECIPES)
5¼ OZ (**150 G**) SMOKED EEL CARCASSES
TAPIOCA FLOUR

Open the oysters, place on a baking sheet covered with baking paper, and cook in a Rational CombiMaster for 90 seconds at 180 °C (82 °C). Marinate in the agave nectar, place them on a Silpat baking mat, and dehydrate in an Excalibur Dehydrator for 4 days at 131 °F (55 °C). Process to a powder in a Thermomix. Combine the remaining ingredients apart from the tapioca. Stir in the oyster powder, bring to a boil, and simmer for 5 minutes. Thicken the sauce with tapioca flour.

GAI LAN:

4½ CUPS (**1 L**) BROCCOLI JUICE
2 TBSP (**30 ML**) CORNISH SEA SALT
4 TBSP (**60 G**) SUGAR
20 HONG KONG GAI LANS,
CUT INTO 1¼ **IN** (**3 CM**) PIECES

Bring the broccoli juice to a boil with the salt and the sugar, then add the gai lan and blanch à la minute.

GAI LAN PUREE:

2 LB 3¼ OZ (**1 KG**) GAI LAN
3 CUPS (**1 LB 1½ OZ/500 G**) ROMANESCO
3 TBSP (**45 ML**) GREEN CHILI SAUCE
(→ SEE BASIC RECIPES)
2 TBSP (**30 ML**) GARLIC OIL
(→ SEE BASIC RECIPES)
2 TBSP (**30 ML**) TABASCO GREEN PEPPER SAUCE
CORNISH SEA SALT
A FEW PINCHES OF XANTHAN GUM

In a saucepan, cook the gai lan and the Romanesco in salted water until they disintegrate. Transfer to a Thermomix and process to a smooth puree.
Add all the remaining ingredients to the puree and process in the Thermomix to a blancmange-like consistency. Transfer to a spray bottle.

LIME TAPIOCA:

⅔ CUP (**100 G**) SMALL GREEN TAPIOCA PEARLS, COOKED UNTIL SOFT
FINELY GRATED ZEST OF **1** LIME
3 TBSP (**45 ML**) LIME JUICE
1 TBSP (**15 ML**) ROSE'S LEMON CORDIAL

Stir all the ingredients together and chill.

GARNISH:

FOR EACH PERSON …
3 SLICES OF YOUNG GINGER
(→ SEE BASIC RECIPES)
2 NASTURTIUM LEAVES

SHRIMP, TOMATO & GALANGAL

There are many kinds of red shrimp, but I'll never forget the dark red Carabineros, or cardinal shrimp, which I first tried during a brief stint working in Mallorca. Firm to the bite, slightly sweet, with a long-lasting aroma, they were rather highly priced even then. The finger-sized red shrimp we use in this recipe also come from Spain, but they are sweeter, their texture is softer, and you simply quick-fry them on the front and the back. You can also enjoy them on their own, just with some pa amb oli (bread with olive oil) and a splotch of aioli. This is a delicious way to eat them at home. In the restaurant, we serve them with a sophisticated Asian note.

SHRIMP:

20 RED SHRIMP, SHELLED AND DEVEINED
4 TBSP (60 ML) GARLIC OIL
(→ SEE BASIC RECIPES)
CORNISH SEA SALT

Marinate the shrimp in the garlic oil and fry for 90 seconds on each side. Season with salt and serve straightaway.

TOMATO COMPOTE WITH GALANGAL:

2¾ CUPS (500 G) HONEYTOMATOES®
⅔ CUP (30 G) GALANGAL, VERY FINELY DICED
2 TBSP (30 ML) HOT BANANA SAUCE
2 TBSP (30 ML) RED CHILI SAUCE
(→ SEE BASIC RECIPES)
2 TBSP (30 ML) RICE VINEGAR
2 TSP (10 G) BONE SUCKIN' HABANERO SAUCE
XANTHAN GUM

Blanch the tomatoes and rinse in iced water. Remove the skins then finely chop the flesh.
Stir all the remaining ingredients apart from the xanthan gum into the tomato pieces. Let infuse for 12 hours, then put into a strainer. Let the liquid drain, catching it in a bowl. Thicken the liquid was a little xanthan, return to the tomatoes, and stir to combine.

MERINGUE:

7 TBSP (100 ML) WATER
⅓ CUP PLUS 2 TBSP (100 G) SUGAR
2 TBSP (25 G) EGG WHITE POWDER
1 TBSP (15 ML) SHICHIMI TOGARASHI SPICE MIXTURE
1 CUP (40 G) SMALL PIECES OF SHRIMP CHIPS

In a KitchenAid, beat the water, sugar, egg white powder, and shichimi to make a meringue mixture. Place round dots of the mixture onto a Silpat baking mat. Top the meringue dots with the shrimp chip pieces, then dehydrate them in an Excalibur Dehydrator for 12 hours at 131 °F (55 °C).

GARNISH:

FOR EACH PERSON ...
½ SLICE OF KUMQUAT
2 SMALL THAI BASIL LEAVES
2 DOTS OF SHELLFISH MAYONNAISE
(→ SEE BASIC RECIPES)

LOBSTER, CARROT & BUTTER

It's always rather hard to like all dishes equally. I usually try to explain to my guests that every dish is like a child, and even if you have ten children, you'll never say that Child Number Three is much cleverer than the others, or that you love Child Number Nine most of all — even if this is the case. Thus, for me, this lobster dish is something really special. It was created in the year when we received our second *Michelin* star, and it clearly indicates the progress we made during that year. The dishes had become more elegant, and since then have featured a finesse which had previously been hidden by an excess of spices. The aromatic characteristics have also become more complex since, by focusing totally on a main component, with the accompaniments highlighting this main ingredient from several sides.

LOBSTER:

2½ GALLONS (10 L) WATER
CORNISH SEA SALT
5 EUROPEAN BLUE LOBSTERS, **1 LB 9 OZ–1 LB 12 OZ (600–800 G)** EACH
5 TBSP (80 ML) RED CHILI SAUCE
(→ SEE BASIC RECIPES)
JAPANESE AONORI PAPRIKA POWDER
3 TBSP (40 ML) CLARIFIED BUTTER

In a large saucepan, bring the water to a boil, add the salt and the lobsters. Make sure the lobsters are immediately submerged in the boiling water so that they die quickly. Take the saucepan off the heat and let the lobsters cook for 3 minutes. Take out the lobsters and rinse in iced water. Break off the pincers and the joints, return to the water, and boil for another 3 minutes. Then remove, devein, halve, and wash the flesh.
Flavor the lobster flesh with the red chili sauce, aomori powder, and Cornish sea salt. Keep warm in a Lohberger Cook'n'Hold for 30 minutes at 156 °F (69 °C) in a little clarified butter.

DASHI VINEGAR JELLY:

7 TBSP (100 ML) DASHI
(→ SEE BASIC RECIPES)
4 TBSP (60 ML) MUSHI SAUCE
(→ SEE BASIC RECIPES)
4 TBSP (60 ML) RICE VINEGAR
½ TBSP (2 G) AGAR AGAR POWDER

In a sauté pan, bring the liquids to a boil. Stir in the agar agar and simmer for 5 minutes. Transfer to a Thermomix bowl and let cool, then process to a smooth jelly. Transfer to a spray bottle.

CARROT PUREE:

4 CUPS (600 G) PEELED AND SLICED CARROTS
10 TBSP (150 ML) LIQUID CLARIFIED BUTTER
2 CUPS (100 G) PEELED AND FINELY DICED GINGER
4 TBSP (60 ML) RED CHILI SAUCE
(→ SEE BASIC RECIPES)
4 TBSP (60 ML) ORANGE OIL
4 TBSP (60 ML) SRIRACHA SAUCE
MUSCOVADO SUGAR
CORNISH SEA SALT

Put all the ingredients apart from the sugar and the salt into a saucepan, cover with a lid, and sauté until the carrots are cooked. Puree in a Thermomix, then season the puree with the muscovado sugar and the Cornish sea salt.

GARNISH:

FOR EACH PERSON …
4 CILANTRO STEMS
3 SLICES OF GINGER, **¼ × ¼ IN (5 × 5 MM)**
1 ESPRESSO SPOON (2.5 ML) PASSION FRUIT SEEDS
2 TBSP (30 ML) LIQUID CLARIFIED BUTTER

SPINY LOBSTER, PONDICHERRY PEPPER, WASABI ARUGULA & LITCHI

In the past, at the Swissôtel Berlin Restaurant 44, combining spiny lobster, litchi, and rose brought me lots of publicity; other starred chefs and restaurant critics enthused about this combination. Here you'll find a further development of the dish. Even for us, obtaining live Breton spiny lobsters is a logistical and financial challenge. Once you have tried it, however, you'll probably agree with me that it is well worth the effort.

SPINY LOBSTER:

10 QUARTS PLUS 3½ CUPS (10 L) SALTED WATER
5 BRETON SPINY LOBSTERS, **14 OZ (400 G)** EACH
10 TBSP (150 ML) CLARIFIED BUTTER
CORNISH SEA SALT

In a large saucepan, bring the salted water to a boil and add the spiny lobsters. Make sure the lobsters are immediately submerged in the boiling water so that they die quickly. Take the saucepan off the heat and let the lobsters cook for another 20 minutes. Take the lobsters out of the saucepan and rinse in iced water. Now remove the flesh from the carcasses, devein, halve, and wash it. Coat the spiny lobster flesh with clarified butter, season with Cornish sea salt, and keep warm in a Lohberger Cook'n'Hold for 30 minutes at 156 °F (69 °C).

PONDICHERRY PEPPER CREAM:

3½ TBSP (20 G) PONDICHERRY PINK PEPPERCORNS
½ CUP (125 ML) MILK
⅔ CUP (150 G) HEAVY CREAM
3 TBSP (40 G) RASPBERRY PUREE
13 TBSP (200 G) PHILADELPHIA CREAM CHEESE
AGAVE NECTAR
CORNISH SEA SALT

In a sauté pan, bring the peppercorns, milk, and cream to a boil and reduce to one-third. Transfer the mixture to a Thermomix and process for 2 minutes at Speed 4, then strain through a fine-mesh strainer. Stir in the raspberry puree and the Philadelphia cream cheese.
Flavor the cream to taste with agave nectar and Cornish sea salt, then transfer to a spray bottle.

LITCHI JELLY:

2 CUPS PLUS 1½ TBSP (500 ML) LITCHI JUICE
1 CUP (250 ML) ROSE'S LEMON CORDIAL
1 CUP (250 ML) WATER
A TRACE OF CITRAS POWDER (TRISODIUM CITRATE)
A TRACE OF BEETROOT POWDER
1½ OZ (40 G) ELASTIC POWDER

Put all the ingredients apart from the elastic powder into a saucepan and bring to a boil. Stir the elastic powder into the boiling broth, take off the heat, and let cool. Pour the mixture onto a GN tray and chill for 2 hours. Cut the jelly into 4 × 4 in (10 × 10 cm) squares.

LITCHI COMPOTE:

10 LITCHIS, SHELLED AND FLESH FINELY DICED
1 TBSP (15 G) PEELED AND VERY FINELY DICED GINGER
1 TSP (5 G) ROSE JELLY

Combine all the ingredients and shape into ten quenelles.

GARNISH:

FOR EACH PERSON …
3 WASABI ARUGULA LEAVES
4 SLICES OF SWEET AND SOUR RADISH

DRUNKEN SHRIMP

I was first served drunken shrimp at the East Coast Seafood Centre in Singapore. Many stories are woven around this dish. One of them tells of freshwater shrimp that were to be eaten raw being preserved in alcohol to make them easier to digest. I like the East Coast version much better: Small shrimp were taken straight from the aquarium and put into a hot wok, to which garlic oil and a shot of Hennessy XO cognac were added. A very "immediate" dish, which cannot be cooked the same way in countries like Germany where live prawns are not traded.

SHRIMP:

3½ TBSP (50 ML) GARLIC OIL
(→ SEE BASIC RECIPES)
14 OZ (400 G) JAPANESE ARCTIC SEA SHRIMP, SHELLED AND DEVEINED
CORNISH SEA SALT
4 PINCHES OF JAPANESE AOMORI PAPRIKA

Heat a wok. Add the oil, then immediately add and sauté the shrimp. Take out the shrimp, place them on paper towels, and season immediately with salt and aomori to taste.

COGNAC GEL:

1½ CUPS PLUS 1 TBSP (375 ML) HENNESSY XO COGNAC
2 CUPS PLUS 1½ TBSP (500 ML) COCA-COLA
SEEDS OF **1** VANILLA BEAN
2 TBSP (25 G) MUSCOVADO SUGAR
2 TBSP (8 G) AGAR AGAR POWDER

In a sauté pan, bring 11⅓ cups plus 2 tablespoons (350 ml) cognac and the Coca-Cola, vanilla seeds, and sugar to a boil. Stir in the agar agar powder and simmer for 5 minutes. Transfer the mixture to a Thermomix bowl and let cool, then process to a smooth gel. Stir in the remaining 2 tablespoons (25 ml) of cognac. Transfer the gel to a spray bottle.

GARNISH:

FOR EACH PERSON ...
1 DOT OF SHELLFISH MAYONNAISE
(→ SEE BASIC RECIPES)
A PINCH OF WAKAME SEAWEED

CAVIAR & BERLIN MUSTARD EGG

In the spring of 2013, we opened La Soupe Populaire Tim Raue Restaurant in the grounds of the former Bötzow brewery in Berlin for Professor Hans-Georg Näder. He had asked me for a gastronomic concept that would be accessible to everyone — in financial as well as in culinary terms. I have been working with Michael Jaeger, the head of kitchen there, since 2003. As native Berliners, we had long been discussing how we could create a restaurant that would serve solely the cuisines of Berlin and Prussia.

In the summer of that same year, the German Chancellor Angela Merkel requested we cook the official state banquet in honor of then U.S. President Barack Obama, and she expressly demanded a menu from the La Soupe Populaire Tim Raue, not from the Restaurant Tim Raue. Thus began the triumphal march of the restaurant, and especially of our Königsberger Klopse (Königsberg meatballs). The first example of this contemporary interpretation of Berlin and Prussian dishes, however, was my version of the Berliner Senfei (Berlin mustard egg), which I created in 2002.

EGGS:

10 EGGS, MEDIUM-BOILED AND SHELLED

BEET SALAD:

3 CUPS (400 G) COOKED BEETS
4 TBSP (80 G) REDCURRANT JELLY
5 TBSP (80 ML) RASPBERRY VINEGAR
2 PICKLED JALAPEÑO PEPPERS
FRESHLY GROUND WHITE PEPPER

Shave the beets into thin slices. Puree the remaining ingredients for 30 seconds at Speed 4 in a Thermomix. Combine with the beet shavings, and put into a vacuum bag. Vacuumize and let infuse for 24 hours. Take the beet shavings out of the bag and arrange in ten piles.

MUSTARD FOAM:

1¼ CUPS (300 ML) CHICKEN BROTH
14 TBSP (200 G) HEAVY CREAM
⅔ STICK (**⅓ CUP/70 G**) BUTTER
3 TBSP (45 ML) BAUTZ'NER MUSTARD
2 TBSP (30 ML) JAPANESE MUSTARD
2 TBSP (30 ML) HÄNDLMAIER SWEET BAVARIAN MUSTARD
CORNISH SEA SALT
CORNSTARCH

In a sauté pan, bring the chicken broth to a boil with the cream, butter, and the three types of mustard. Season with salt and thicken well with the cornstarch. Strain through a fine-mesh strainer and transfer to an iSi thermo whip. Fit the flask with two cream chargers and keep warm.

GARNISH:

FOR EACH PERSON ...
1 TBSP (15 G) IMPERIAL CAVIAR
1 TBSP (20 G) POTATO PUREE
1 STALK CHERVIL
2 POTATO CHIPS MADE FROM NEW POTATOES

poultry

When I think of poultry, an image appears in my mind's eye of the fried chicken stall outside Görlitzer Station in Berlin. Crisp, brown broilers, steaming and juicy, were cut in half, and I greedily tore the meat off the bones with my fingers. I devoured the giblets especially with the greatest delight. I preferred the juicy meat of the legs to that of the breast, and today you can still tempt me more with poultry than with any other meat.

I am particularly fond of Chinese barbecue dishes, when whole pigeons or chickens are glazed with marinades, dried, and finally deep-fried until crispy. The German classic of roast goose is not my thing, but I'll drop everything for a roast duck with red cabbage and dumplings.

For years, my version of the Peking Duck was my signature dish, which defined me and which is also included in this book in an updated form.

At the Singaporean Crystal Jade Palace Restaurant I first ate a beggar's chicken, which I shall never forget.

Unfortunately, poultry does not enjoy a good reputation in Germany, and chicken especially is not rated nearly as highly as it is in Asia.

PEKING DUCK

Restaurant Tim Raue is unimaginable without its Peking Duck. We serve it on three plates. The prominent component is not only the skin, as in the original version, but the entire duck: A duck liver mousse with cucumber, leek, and crispy skin, a duck broth with giblets — tongue, heart, and gizzards —, as well as a fried duck breast with leeks, apple, and a duck feet sauce. Below you'll find the recipes — take plenty of time and enjoy the cooking process.

PLATE I, DUCK BREAST:

5 DUCK BREASTS
3 TBSP (45 ML) MALTOSE SYRUP
FAT FOR FRYING
CORNISH SEA SALT

Remove any tendons from the duck breasts. Brush the skin side with hot water until the skin swells up and glistens.
Heat the maltose and cover the duck breasts with it. Dry in front of a ventilator for 4 hours on a medium setting.
Sear the duck breasts on both sides, then roast them in the oven for 3 minutes at 356 °F (180 °C) convection. Take out and place in a Lohberger Cook'n'Hold drawer for 1 hour at 156 °F (69 °C).
On a griddle, fry the skin side of the duck breasts until crispy. Season with Cornish sea salt.

DUCK FEET SAUCE:

2 LB 3¼ OZ (1 KG) DUCK LEGS, LIGHTLY ROASTED IN THE OVEN AT **392 °F (200 °C)**
14 OZ (400 G) DUCK FEET, CLEANED AND DEEP-FRIED
1 CUP (250 ML) RICE WINE
½ CUP PLUS 1 TBSP (175 G) LEE KUM KEE CHAR SIU SAUCE
½ CUP PLUS 1 TBSP (175 G) LEE KUM KEE PEKING DUCK SAUCE
14 TBSP (200 ML) MUSHI SAUCE
(→ SEE BASIC RECIPES)
1 CUP PLUS 1½ TBSP (200 G) MUSCOVADO SUGAR
14 TBSP (200 ML) GREEN CHILI SAUCE
(→ SEE BASIC RECIPES)
1 TBSP (15 ML) TABASCO GREEN PEPPER SAUCE
⅔ CUP (100 G) PEELED AND FINELY DICED CARROTS
1 CUP (100 G) FINELY DICED CELERY
⅓ CUP (50 G) PEELED AND FINELY DICED ONIONS
CORNSTARCH

Put all the ingredients apart from the cornstarch into a saucepan, bring to a boil and simmer for 1 hour. Strain through a chinois bouillon strainer and thicken with the cornstarch.

DUCK SKIN CRACKLING:

13¼ OZ (375 G) DUCK SKIN
2 CUPS PUS 1½ TBSP (500 ML) RICE WINE
4 TBSP (40 G) CORNISH SEA SALT
8 CUPS (2 L) WATER
1¾ CUPS (225 G) TAPIOCA FLOUR
8⅓ CUPS (250 G) PUFFED QUINOA
2½ CUPS (300 G) CONFECTIONERS' SUGAR
14 TBSP (100 G) FIVE-SPICE POWDER
FAT FOR DEEP-FRYING

Put the duck skin together with the rice wine, salt, and water into a saucepan and bring to a boil. Simmer for 5 hours, adding 1 cup (250 ml) water after every hour of cooking.
Put the duck skin, 3 cups 1½ tablespoons (750 ml) of the broth, and the tapioca flour into a Thermomix and process for 5 minutes on Speed 10 to a smooth mixture. Set the Thermomix to 212 °F (100 °C) and run for 12 minutes on Speed 3. Pass the mixture through a strainer and spread onto Silpat baking mats. Sprinkle over the quinoa, then dehydrate the mixture in an Excalibur Dehydrator for 45 minutes at 176 °F (80 °C). Cut into ½ × 1 in (1.5 × 2.5 cm) rectangles.
Combine the confectioners' sugar and the five-spice powder, and put them into a fine-mesh strainer. In a deep-fryer, briefly deep-fry the duck skin rectangles in the fat heated to 356 °F (180 °C). Remove, place onto paper towels and pat dry. Divide the duck skin between baking sheets, and dust with the sugar and spice mix. Briefly hold in a salamander until the sugar has caramelized. Store in a dry place.

LEEK AND APPLE ROLLS:

10 TBSP (55 G) LEEK, FINELY CHOPPED AND SAUTÉED IN A WOK IN A LITTLE GARLIC OIL
3½ TBSP (50 ML) APPLESAUCE
10 SLICES OF LEEK, SLICED LENGTHWAYS, **2½ × 2¾ IN (6 × 7 CM)**, BRIEFLY BLANCHED

Combine the sautéed leeks and the applesauce. Spread a little of the mixture onto the long sides of the leek slices, then carefully roll up the leeks.

PEKING DUCK

continued

PLATE 2, DUCK BROTH: DUCK GIBLETS:

5 DUCK HEARTS, CLEANED AND QUARTERED
FAT FOR SAUTÉING
10 DUCK TONGUES
10 DUCK GIZZARDS, CLEANED
VEGETABLE OIL
1¼ **CUPS (300 ML)** VEGETABLE OIL
CORNISH SEA SALT
6 TBSP (90 ML) PLUM SAUCE FOR PEKING DUCK (→ SEE BASIC RECIPES)

Briefly sauté the duck hearts in a wok. Vacuumize the duck tongues, then steam in a Rational CombiMaster for 3 hours at 180°F (82°C). Remove the cartilage from the warm tongues and discard. Season the gizzards with salt. Heat the oil to 194°F (90°C), then cook the gizzards in it for 3 hours.
Marinate all the giblets in the plum sauce and keep warm in a Lohberger Cook'n'Hold for 15 minutes at 156°F (69°C).

SOUP GARNISHES:

2 CUPS (300 G) PEELED AND DESEEDED WINTER MELON
7 TBSP (100 ML) DUCK BROTH (→ SEE BASIC RECIPES)
5 BAMBOO FUNGI
2 CUPS (200 G) CHOPPED CELERY
4½ **CUPS (1 L)** DUCK BROTH (→ SEE BASIC RECIPES)

Vacuumize the winter melon with the duck broth and steam in a Rational CombiMaster for 20 minutes at 180°F (82°C). Let cool, then finely dice the melon. Soak the fungi for 1 hour in lukewarm water, then take out and cut into slices.
Combine all the soup garnishes and divide between bowls. Fill the bowls with the hot duck broth.

PLATE 3, DUCK LIVER MOUSSE:

12¼ **OZ (350 G)** DUCK LIVER
⅔ **CUP (150 G)** HEAVY CREAM
4 TBSP (60 ML) PLUM SAUCE FOR PEKING DUCK (→ SEE BASIC RECIPES)
5 LEAVES GELATIN, SOAKED IN COLD WATER
CORNISH SEA SALT
1½ **CUPS (170 G)** WHIPPED CREAM

In a saucepan, heat the duck liver with the cream and the plum sauce until the liver has dissolved. Heat the gelatin to dissolve, then stir in. Season the mousse with salt, take off the heat, and let cool to room temperature. Fold in the whipped cream, divide the mousse between 2-in-(5-cm)-diameter semi-circular molds and chill. Let set for 3 hours.

GARNISH:

FOR EACH PERSON ...
3 DOTS OF GINGER AND LEEK PUREE (→ SEE BASIC RECIPES)
3 DOTS OF PLUM SAUCE FOR PEKING DUCK (→ SEE BASIC RECIPES)
3 CUCUMBER BALLS, SHAPED WITH A MELON BALLER, MARINATED IN RICE VINEGAR
3 DILL FRONDS

SICHUAN PIGEON

The Sichuan region of China is known for its spicy food and the exuberant use of oils and fats. At first glance this may not sound very attractive, yet the Sichuan hot pot in particular, as well as the dishes containing roasted chiles, are often magnificent. The use of Sichuan pepper, which is not actually a pepper but a citrus plant, determines the aromas in Sichuan cuisine.

The spiciness has the same effect as a laser sword — it simultaneously brightens the palate and lights it up with a searing heat. Please therefore exercise caution when using Sichuan pepper; dishes that have been excessively spiced cannot be rescued — and moreover cannot be eaten.

PIGEON:

10 WHOLE PIGEONS, GUTTED
10 STRIPS OF DRIED CHINESE MANDARIN ORANGE ZEST
4 TBSP (60 ML) ORANGE OIL (→ SEE BASIC RECIPES)
CORNISH SEA SALT
5 TSP (25 ML) FINELY GRATED MANDARIN ORANGE ZEST

Vacuumize the pigeons individually with 1 strip of mandarin zest each and cook over a bain-marie for 1 hour at 136 °F (58 °C). Remove the pigeons from the bags, cut off the breasts and remove the skins.
Sear the pigeon breasts on both sides in orange oil, season with salt, and sprinkle the tops with the grated mandarin zest.

TAMARIND SAUCE:

8 CUPS (2 L) BEEF TEA (→ SEE BASIC RECIPES)
10 PIGEON CARCASSES
6 TBSP (100 G) SEEDLESS TAMARIND PASTE
⅓ CUP (50 G) PALM SUGAR
2 TBSP (30 ML) BONE SUCKIN' HABANERO SAUCE
3 TBSP (45 ML) CHINESE FERMENTED BLACK BEANS
4 TBSP (60 ML) ROASTED SICHUAN CHILES, IN OIL
½ ESPRESSO SPOON (1.25 ML) GROUND SICHUAN PEPPERCORNS
4 TBSP (45 G) MUSCOVADO SUGAR

In a saucepan, bring the beef tea, pigeon carcasses, tamarind paste, palm sugar, and habanero sauce to a boil and simmer for 15 minutes, stirring constantly. Strain the sauce through a fine-mesh strainer.
Bring 4½ cups (1 l) of the sauce to a boil with the remaining ingredients, then puree for 2 minutes with a hand blender.

SWEET 'N' SOUR SQUASH:

20 STRIPS OF RED KURI SQUASH, **¾ IN (2 CM)** WIDE AND **6¼ IN (16 CM)**
7 TBSP (100 ML) D'ARBO PASSION FRUIT AND APRICOT SYRUP
7 TBSP (100 ML) RICE VINEGAR

Put all the ingredients into a vacuum bag and vacuumize, then let infuse for 4 hours.

GARNISH:

FOR EACH PERSON …
2 MANDARIN ORANGE SEGMENTS, FILLETED
2 BUNCHES OF WATERCRESS
2 TSP (10 ML) THAI VINAIGRETTE FOR MARINATING (→ SEE BASIC RECIPES)
2 LITTLE **PIECES** OF CANDIED GINGER

LEMON CHICKEN

We created this lemon chicken especially for the opening of the Dragonfly by Tim Raue Restaurant in Dubai. Due to the religious customs prevailing there, we will not be using any pork and are focusing mainly on poultry dishes. Christian Singer, my long-standing head chef of Restaurant Tim Raue, has devised this concept for me and and he will also realize it on-site. The lemon chicken is a dish which — like sweet 'n' sour pork — is often made from the cheapest ingredients, especially in the West. Normally it consists of a deep-fried battered chicken, sprinkled with sesame seeds, and served with a clear lemon sauce.
In Hong Kong you can enjoy a dish of wonderfully juicy chicken legs in a deliciously sweet and acidic sauce, especially at the Lung King Heen Restaurant. I hold the restaurant's chef, Chan, in great esteem. We use Amalfi lemons and parsley to add to the aroma of the dish.

LEMON CHICKEN:

10 MAIZE-FED CHICKEN BREASTS
10 TBSP (150 ML) GOOSE FAT
20 ASIAN LIME LEAVES
10 TBSP (150 ML) LEMON OIL
(→ SEE BASIC RECIPES)
CORNISH SEA SALT

Spread the flesh side of the chicken breasts with goose fat and stick 2 Asian lime leaves to each one. Put into vacuum bags and add 1 tablespoon (15 ml) lemon oil to each chicken breast. Vacuumize and cook over a bain-marie for 18 minutes at 147 °F (64 °C). Take the chicken breasts out of the bags, remove the Asian lime leaves and the skins. Keep the chicken warm in a Lohberger Cook'n'Hold at 156 °F (69 °C). Season with salt.

LEMONGRASS & ASIAN LIME:

2 TBSP (30 ML) VERY FINELY CHOPPED LEMONGRASS
2 TBSP (30 ML) VERY FINELY CHOPPED ASIAN LIME LEAVES

Combine the lemongrass and the Asian lime leaves, then sprinkle the top side of the chicken breasts with the mixture.

SALT & SUGAR:

2 TBSP (20 G) SMOKED MALDON SEA SALT
2 TBSP (20 G) MUSCOVADO SUGAR

Combine the salt and the sugar, then sprinkle the top side of the chicken breasts with the mixture.

LEMON ZEST:

20 STRIPS OF AMALFI LEMON ZEST, EACH MEASURING **1¼ IN (3 CM)** LONG AND **⅛ IN (3 MM)** WIDE
10 TBSP (150 ML) SUGAR SYRUP

Blanch the zests twice in salted water. Bring the sugar syrup to a boil, add the zests, and simmer for 5 minutes. Take off the heat and let cool.

DASHI TAPIOCA:

4½ CUPS (1 L) DASHI (→ SEE BASIC RECIPES)
⅔ CUP (100 G) SMALL WHITE TAPIOCA PEARLS
FAT FOR DEEP-FRYING
CORNISH SEA SALT

Bring the dashi to a boil, add the tapioca pearls and cook until done. Strain the liquid and spread the pearls onto a Silpat baking mat. Dehydrate in an Excalibur Dehydrator for 12 hours at 131 °F (55 °C). Break the tapioca into chunks, Deep-fry in fat heated to 320 °F (160 °C). Put onto paper towels and pat dry, then season with salt. Break into 1¼ × 1½ in (3 × 4 cm) pieces. Store in a dry place.

LEMON SAUCE:

4½ CUPS (1 L) CHICKEN BROTH
(→ SEE BASIC RECIPES)
1⅔ CUPS (400 ML) ROSE'S LEMON CORDIAL
7 TBSP (100 ML) AMALFI LEMON JUICE
1 STALK LEMONGRASS, VERY FINELY CHOPPED
1 GREEN THAI CHILE, THINLY SLICED
¼ CUP (50 G) MUSCOVADO SUGAR
3½ TBSP (50 ML) ELDERFLOWER SYRUP

Put all the ingredients into a sauté pan and cook to reduce by half. Strain through a fine-mesh strainer.

GARNISH:

FOR EACH PERSON ...
1 LARGE **DOT** OF PARSLEY CREAM
(→ SEE BASIC RECIPES)
1 DOT OF CRÈME FRAÎCHE
3 STEMS OF PERSINETTE® CRESS

BEGGAR'S GUINEA FOWL

The dish known as "beggar's chicken" goes back to a Chinese legend, in which a beggar steals a chicken. To hide the bird, he covers and cooks it in clay so that nobody can see he is preparing a chicken. The dish is rather laborious to make and, accordingly, it is celebrated at very good Chinese restaurants with a lot of hoo-ha. Usually, a boned chicken is stuffed with cooked rice and spices. The chicken is first wrapped in aromatic lotus leaves and then covered in clay and cooked in the oven for up to 6 hours. At the table, the clay is split open and the tender, disintegrating chicken and the juicy rice are plated. For me, the decisive aroma comes from the dried lotus leaves; they have a truly unique flavor.

LOTUS LEAF PASTE:

10 DRIED LOTUS LEAVES
⅔ CUP (150 ML) VEGETABLE OIL
1 TBSP (10 G) CORNISH SEA SALT

Combine all the ingredients in a Thermomix and process to a paste.

LOTUS LEAF OIL:

10 DRIED LOTUS LEAVES
2 CUPS (500 ML) VEGETABLE OIL
1 TBSP (10 G) CORNISH SEA SALT

Combine all the ingredients in a Thermomix and puree for 4 minutes on Speed 10. Vacuumize and keep warm over a bain-marie for 4 hours at 156 °F (69 °C), then let cool. Repeat the process four times. Finally let infuse for 24 hours, then strain the oil through a fine muslin cloth.

GUINEA FOWL:

10 GUINEA FOWL LEGS, SKIN AND BONES REMOVED, FREED FROM TENDONS

Spread the guinea fowl legs with the lotus leaf paste and vacuumize.
Let infuse for 36 hours. Take the legs out of the vacuum bags, wash, and pat dry with paper towels. Heat a little of the lotus oil (SEE LEFT) in a skillet and sear the legs on both sides over a high heat for about 30 seconds. Finally, cook in a Lohberger Cook'n'Hold for 30 minutes at 156 °F (69 °C).

SAUCE:

3½ TBSP (50 ML) ZHENJIANG VINEGAR
3½ TBSP (50 ML) GEGENBAUER NOBLE-SOUR P.X. VINEGAR
3½ TBSP (50 ML) BEEF TEA (→ SEE BASIC RECIPES)
3½ TBSP (50 ML) MAPLE SYRUP
1 RED THAI CHILE
1 TBSP (10 G) CORNISH SEA SALT
XANTHAN GUM

Combine all the ingredients apart from the xanthan in a Thermomix and puree for 2 minutes on Speed 8. Add a little xanthan and thicken the liquid to a syrupy consistency, then strain through a fine-mesh strainer.

BEGGAR'S GUINEA FOWL

continued

MUSHROOM PUREE:

3 TBSP (40 G) CLARIFIED BUTTER
5⅓ CUPS (400 G) SLICED CREMINI MUSHROOMS
3 TBSP (45 ML) GARLIC OIL
2 TBSP (30 ML) CHEF SAUCE (→ SEE BASIC RECIPES)
FRESHLY GROUND WHITE PEPPER
XANTHAN GUM

Heat the butter in a skillet, add the mushrooms, and fry over high heat. Add garlic oil and chef sauce, cover with a lid, and sauté for 7 minutes, until the mushrooms are soft. Put everything apart from the pepper and the xanthan into a Thermomix and process to a smooth mixture. Season with white pepper and thicken the mixture with a little xanthan to a puree.

JERUSALEM ARTICHOKE PEEL:

PEEL FROM **2** JERUSALEM ARTICHOKES
OIL FOR DEEP-FRYING

Wash and pat dry the peel. Heat the oil in a deep-fryer, add the peel, and deep-fry for 70 seconds. Place on a Silpat baking mat and dehydrate in an Excalibur Dehydrator overnight at 131 °F (55 °C).

MÂCHE BALLS, BASIC MIXTURE:

9 OZ (250 G) MÂCHE
3 TBSP (30 G) MUSCOVADO SUGAR
1 TBSP (15 ML) MUSTARD
14 TBSP (200 ML) DASHI (→ SEE BASIC RECIPES)
14 TBSP (200 ML) RICE VINEGAR
7 TBSP (100 ML) VEGETABLE OIL
½ ESPRESSO SPOON (1.5 G) CALCIC MOLECULAR POWDER
¼ TSP (1.1 G) XANTHAN GUM

For the mâche basic mixture, put all the ingredients apart from the calcic and the xanthan into a Thermomix and puree for 4 minutes on Speed 10. Put 7 oz (200 g) of the basic mixture together with the calcic and the xanthan into the Thermomix and puree for 30 seconds on Speed 4. Strain through a cheesecloth, then transfer to round chocolate molds and freeze.

ALGINATE SPHERIFICATION BATH:

½ TBSP (10 G) SODIUM ALGINATE
½ TSP (2.4 G) SODIUM CITRATE
1¾ CUPS (400 G) SUGAR
8 CUPS (2 L) WATER

Combine all the ingredients and vacuumize them, then let infuse in a fridge for 2 hours at 39 °F (4 °C).

Pour the liquid into a bowl. Add the frozen mâche balls (SEE LEFT) to the alginate bath and gently move around with a spatula for 30 seconds. Strain the balls in a strainer and rinse under running water for 30 seconds. Keep the mâche balls in the remaining basic mixture until ready to eat.

GARNISH:

FOR EACH PERSON ...
3 DOTS OF RED CHILI COMPOTE (→ SEE BASIC RECIPES)
3 SLICES OF RADISH, CUT INTO A STAR SHAPE
3 HORN OF PLENTY MUSHROOMS, FRIED IN GARLIC OIL (→ SEE BASIC RECIPES)
3 SHIMEJI MUSHROOMS, FRIED IN GARLIC OIL (→ SEE BASIC RECIPES)
6 SMALL MÂCHE LEAVES

SATAY GUINEA FOWL, MANGO & CUCUMBER

Broiled chicken with peanut sauce, originally from Thailand where it is known as saté gai, has become a truly global dish. I find the saté gai at the Moon Thai Restaurant in Berlin simply fantastic. Here, in an adptation of the classic, a broiled guinea fowl is served with peanut sauce and an authentic salad of cucumber and red shallots with rice vinegar. Our recipe is technically a little more demanding and more complex in its aroma, but I nevertheless visit the Moon Thai several times a week.

SATAY GUINEA FOWL:

10 GUINEA FOWL LEGS, SKIN, BONES, AND TENDONS REMOVED
7 TBSP (100 ML) RICE WINE
7 TBSP (100 ML) CHICKEN BROTH (→ SEE BASIC RECIPES)
6 ASIAN LIME LEAVES, FINELY CHOPPED
3½ TBSP (50 ML) MEGACHEF PREMIUM FISH SAUCE
3 TBSP (50 G) LEE KUM KEE CHAR SIU SAUCE
3 TBSP (30 G) MUSCOVADO SUGAR
1 RED THAI CHILE
2 TBSP (30 ML) VERY FINELY CHOPPED LEMONGRASS

Using a scalpel, make dozens of wafer-thin incisions into the sides of the legs. Combine all the remaining ingredients in a Thermomix and process for 4 minutes on Speed 10 to make a marinade. Brush the legs with one-third of the marinade, put into a vacuum bag, vacuumize, and let marinate for 12 hours. Sear the legs on both sides over high heat on a charcoal broiler, then cook in a Lohberger Cook'n'Hold for 30 minutes at 156 °F (69 °C). Use the remaining marinade as a sauce.

PEANUT CREAM:

¾ CUP (200 G) PEANUT BUTTER
7 TBSP (100 ML) CHICKEN BROTH (→ SEE BASIC RECIPES)
2 TBSP (30 ML) GREEN CHILI SAUCE (→ SEE BASIC RECIPES)
2 TBSP (30 ML) OYSTER SAUCE
CORNISH SEA SALT
XANTHAN GUM

In a saucepan, combine the peanut butter, the chicken broth, and the sauces, and bring to a boil. Stir until smooth and season with salt. Add the xanthan and thicken to a blancmange-like consistency. Let cool and transfer to a spray bottle.

CUCUMBER BALLS:

20 CUCUMBER BALLS, FORMED WITH A PARISIENNE MELON BALLER
4 TBSP (60 ML) RICE VINEGAR
4 TBSP (60 ML) CUCUMBER JUICE

Place all the ingredients into a vacuum bag and vacuumize. Let infuse for 1 hour.

GARNISH:

FOR EACH PERSON ...
1 TSP (5 ML) THAI VINAIGRETTE (→ SEE BASIC RECIPES)
3 WILD JUNGLE PEANUTS
3 LEAVES OF BORAGE CRESS
3 DOTS OF COCONUT AND CILANTRO CREAM (→ SEE BASIC RECIPES)
3 THAI MANGO **BALLS**, SHAPED WITH A PARISIENNE MELON BALLER
4 SLICES OF THAI RED SHALLOTS

MISO CHICKEN, ORANGE & EGGPLANT

Miso chicken is a "Japanized" recipe. Eggplant, miso, and kumquats make for a harmonious ensemble, with red chiles forming a spicy contrast. Eggplant are often combined with miso in Japan; they can be marinated in miso and then deep-fried, or miso mayonnaise and some orange zest can simply be served with the deep-fried eggplant. A 2010 Kirin sake makes the perfect accompaniment.

MISO CHICKEN:

10 MAIZE-FED CHICKEN LEGS, BONED AND PREPARED
4 TBSP (60 ML) ORANGE OIL
(→ SEE BASIC RECIPES)
CORNISH SEA SALT
ORANGE OIL FOR SEARING
(→ SEE BASIC RECIPES)
1½ TBSP (25 ML) SMOKED CHIPOTLE CHILES, MIXED

Place each chicken leg onto a piece of plastic wrap, brush with the orange oil, and generously season with salt. Put the chipotle chiles on the inner sides of the legs, then roll up the plastic wrap to make chicken legs rolls. Place the rolls into vacuum bags, vacuumize, then cook over a bain-marie for 50 minutes at 156 °F (69 °C). Unwrap the rolls and sear in orange oil over high heat.

MISO FOAM:

2 CUPS (500 ML) MILK
⅔ CUP (150 G) HEAVY CREAM
½ CUP (120 G) NUT BUTTER
2 TBSP (30 ML) HÄNDLMAIER SWEET BAVARIAN MUSTARD
2 TBSP (30 ML) LIGHT MISO PASTE
3½ TBSP (50 ML) APPLE JUICE
CORNSTARCH

Combine all the ingredients apart from the cornstarch in a saucepan and bring to a boil. Puree with a hand blender for 1 minute, then strain through a fine-mesh strainer.
Bring the mixture to a boil again, then thicken with the cornstarch. Strain again through a fine-mesh strainer and transfer to an iSi thermo whip. Fit with two cream chargers and keep warm.

EGGPLANT:

5 SLICES OF EGGPLANT, **1¼ IN (3 CM)**
PEANUT OIL FOR DEEP-FRYING
CORNISH SEA SALT

Deep-fry the eggplant slices in the peanut oil heated to 338 °F (170 °C) until bronze in color. Take out the slices, halve, and immediately season with salt.

MISO MAYONNAISE:

4 TBSP (60 ML) JAPANESE MAYONNAISE
1 TSP (5 ML) WHITE MISO PASTE
½ TSP (2.5 ML) JAPANESE MUSTARD
½ TSP (2.5 ML) HÄNDLMAIER SWEET BAVARIAN MUSTARD

Stir all the ingredients together and transfer to a spray bottle.

GARNISH:

FOR EACH PERSON ...
3 CUBES OF JAPANESE YELLOW RADISH, **¼ IN (5 MM)**
1 TBSP (15 ML) YELLOW BEETS, CUT INTO STRIPS WITH A JAPANESE VEGETABLE SLICER
1 TSP (5 ML) MUSTARD SEED, COOKED UNTIL SOFT
1 TSP (5 ML) ORANGE MARMALADE
3 LEAVES OF WASABI ARUGULA

CAPON, ALBA TRUFFLE & SQUASH

In France, the capon — a castrated and fattened rooster — is considered the juiciest and noblest of birds. Every year, we buy a few of them from Bresse at Christmas, so we can cook them whole for New Year's Eve and serve them the traditional way with pumpkin and Alba truffle. Due to its price — a 6.6-lb bird can cost well over 100 dollars — we can only accommodate the capon in our New Year's Eve menu. At other times, it's a disastrous product for the sales balance!

CAPON:

1 WHOLE CAPON
2 STICKS PLUS 2 TBSP (1 CUP PLUS 2 TBSP/250 G) SALTED BUTTER, AT ROOM TEMPERATURE
8 CUPS (2 L) CHICKEN BROTH
(→ SEE BASIC RECIPES)

Gut the capon. Place onto a rack and pour over hot water on all sides three times. Chill. Rub the capon all over with the butter, put it in a vacuum bag and vacuumize, then cook over a bain-marie for 4 hours at 156 °F (69 °C). Take the capon out of the bag and cut away the breast and the legs.
In a sauté pan, reduce the chicken broth to 4 ½ cups (1 liter). Heat the stock to 185 °F (85 °C), add the capon breasts and cook for 6 minutes. Take out and cook in a Lohberger Cook'n'Hold for another 15 minutes at 156 °F (69 °C). Separate the meat from the leg bones and simmer for 15 minutes in the chicken broth.

ALBA TRUFFLE CREAM SAUCE:

⅓ CUP (30 G) SHAVED ALBA TRUFFLES, SHAVED INTO VERY THIN SLICES
1½ TBSP (20 G) LIQUID BUTTER
14 TBSP (200 ML) CHICKEN BROTH
(→ SEE BASIC RECIPES)
3½ TBSP (50 G) HEAVY CREAM
3½ TBSP (50 G) MUSHI SAUCE
(→ SEE BASIC RECIPES)

Stir together the shaved truffles and the butter and let infuse for 24 hours. Put the chicken broth, cream, and mushi sauce into a sauté pan and cook to reduce by half. Stir in the truffle butter.

SQUASH AND MIMOLETTE CREAM:

8½ CUPS (1 KG) PREPARED RED KURI SQUASH, CHOPPED INTO CHUNKS
7 TBSP (100 ML) RED CHILI SAUCE
(→ SEE BASIC RECIPES)
CORNISH SEA SALT
⅔ CUP (150 G) CRÈME FRAÎCHE
2 CUPS (200 G) FINELY GRATED MIMOLETTE CHEESE

Marinate the squash in the chili sauce and salt. Wrap in baking paper, place in a baking pan, and cover with a baking sheet. Bake for 60 minutes in an oven preheated to 350 °F (176 °C) until soft. Transfer everything from the baking paper to a Thermomix and process to a smooth puree.
Stir the crème fraîche and the mimolette into the mixture while still hot. Season with salt.

SWEET 'N' SOUR PUMPKIN:

10 SLICES RED KURI SQUASH, **¾ IN (2 CM)** THICK AND **4 IN (10CM)** LONG
4 TBSP (60 ML) RICE VINEGAR
4 TBSP (60 ML) D'ARBO PASSION FRUIT & MANDARIN ORANGE SYRUP

Put all the ingredients together into a vacuum bag and vacuumize, then let infuse for 24 hours.

GEL OF CHINESE SAUSAGE:

7 OZ (200 G) CHINESE SAUSAGE, THINLY SLICED
1¼ CUP (300 ML) BEEF TEA
(→ SEE BASIC RECIPES)
14 TBSP (200 ML) MUSHI SAUCE
(→ SEE BASIC RECIPES)
1 TBSP (4 G) AGAR AGAR POWDER

In a sauté pan without fat, dry-sear the sausage. Add both liquids and bring to a boil, then simmer for 15 minutes. Strain the liquid, return to the pan, and bring back to a boil. Stir in the agar agar powder and simmer the broth for 5 minutes. Transfer to a Thermomix bowl and let cool, then puree to a smooth gel.

GARNISH:

FOR EACH PERSON ...
1 TBSP CRUSHED GALETTES BRETONNES AUX AMANDES (BRETON ALMOND COOKIES)
1 TBSP (4 G) SHAVED SLICES OF ALBA TRUFFLES, CUT OUT AS DISKS
4 LEAVES OF GROUND ELDER

GOOSE IN BROTH

During my training I had to shift and roast geese, in high season up to 120 birds a day, which I first had to stuff with onions, apples, marzipan, and dried mugwort. It was a traumatic experience, especially because the geese were so large and the oven was really too small to accommodate them. Thus, today, I serve duck for Christmas, and goose doesn't feature on the restaurant's menu.

I did, however, once eat a really funny goose dish, at the Vietnam Center in Berlin Lichtenberg. Shady characters sat at the nearby tables, as my mate Duc ordered soured goose. A gigantic saucepan was brought to the table, with the goose swimming in a vinegary-sour broth and its feet sticking out at the top. We garnered appreciative glances from the guys at the next table, and the first bite revealed why: It was the toughest beast I've had to face during my entire career. Now the Vietnamese are, of course, fantastic soup chefs, and this is why I dedicate this recipe to them, which is set to bring color to the gray life of the everyday goose.

GOOSE:

10 CURED GOOSE LEGS
1 GALLON PLUS ¾ CUPS (4 L) CHICKEN BROTH (→ SEE BASIC RECIPES)
4½ CUPS (1 L) ROSE'S LEMON CORDIAL
½ CUP (50 G) PEELED AND FINELY SLICED GALANGAL
6 FRESH BAY LEAVES
6 GARLIC CLOVES, PEELED
1⅔ CUP (300 G) MUSCOVADO SUGAR
1¼ CUPS (300 ML) PLUM WINE
7 TBSP (100 ML) GEGENBAUER NOBLE-SOUR P.X. VINEGAR

In a saucepan, combine all the ingredients apart from the plum wine and the vinegar, and bring to a boil. Cover with a lid and simmer for 3 hours, until the goose legs are cooked. Strain the broth. Add the plum wine and the vinegar, bring back to a boil, and simmer for another 15 minutes. Strain the sauce through a cheesecloth.

SOUP GARNISHES:

20 WATER CHESTNUTS, COOKED AND DICED
30 SLICES OF GREEN RADISH, SHAVED INTO THIN SLICES
2 PRESERVED PORCINI, SLICED
3½ TBSP (50 ML) SPRING LEEKS, THINLY SLICED
10 TBSP (150 ML) CHIVE OIL (→ SEE BASIC RECIPES)
10 TBSP (150 ML) SMOKED OIL (→ SEE BASIC RECIPES)
1 TBSP (15 ML) PEELED AND VERY FINELY DICED GALANGAL
10 STEMS OF HANA-SANSHO FLOWERS

meat

I've never understood the classic meat dishes of French cuisine. It has always irritated me that, for the main course of a meal, you gobble down a massive piece of meat swimming in a sauce which has been reduced for days, and which gums up your palate within seconds.

There are hardly ever any notes of piquancy to add acidity, sweetness, or heat; a light vegetable accompaniment, or an enlivening salad; let alone pickled vegetables to provide refreshment. I never want to serve anything like that in our restaurants.

This is why we combine our meat courses with the side dishes mentioned above, as well as with acidity, sweetness, and reviving heat. Now meat is not a heavy main course, but part of a balanced meal and the final savory dish.

For me there is nothing more ravishing than a Chinese barbecue. My favorite is Char Siu red roasted pork, which you can buy in Singapore from countless street food stalls, alongside crispy pork belly or a suckling pig marinated in honey.

Visiting food courts, such as Newton in Singapore, where dozens of food stalls are grouped around a central plaza, is a unique experience. Here you can find an unbelievable variety, from local dishes such as rojak, laksa, and chili crab, to Chinese barbecue and dim sums. Singaporeans go here to eat with their friends, and everyone chooses two or three dishes to share with the other diners, turning a simple meal into a veritable festival of delights.

SHABU-SHABU BEEF, LEEK & GINGER

Shabu-shabu is a Japanese method of preparation in which the guests themselves cook thin slices of meat in a hot broth and then immediately eat them. A favorite choice for this dish are cuts of the heavily marbled flesh of Wagyu cattle, such as short loin or sirloin. The two most important components are the aromatic broth and the meat; we also add leeks and a little ginger for extra spice.

WAGYU BEEF:

10 PIECES OF WAGYU BEEF SHORT LOIN OR SIRLOIN, **3 OZ (80 G)** EACH, CUT NTO RECTANGLES

Place the meat in a Lohberger Cook'n'Hold for 90 minutes at 156 °F (69 °C), then cook in the hot shabu-shabu broth (SEE BELOW) for 2 minutes at 194 °F (90 °C). Take the meat out of the broth and cut into thin slices.

SHABU-SHABU BROTH:

4½ CUPS (1 L) BEEF TEA (→ SEE BASIC RECIPES)
7 OZ (200 G) WAGYU BEEF RIB
2 GREEN THAI CHILES, FINELY CHOPPED
½ CUP (120 ML) MUSHI SAUCE, STRAINED (→ SEE BASIC RECIPES)

Combine all the ingredients and bring to a boil, then simmer for 30 minutes. Take off the heat, cook for another 30 minutes. Strain through a cheesecloth. Bring the broth to a boil again, ready for cooking the Wagyu beef slices in it.

LEEK & GINGER:

2 SPRING LEEKS, CUT INTO WAFER-THIN RINGS
2 TBSP (30 ML) VERY FINELY DICED GINGER
1 TBSP (15 ML) GINGER AND LEEK PUREE (→ SEE BASIC RECIPES)

With a mortar and pestle, crush the spring leeks and the ginger to a paste. Combine with the ginger and leek puree, then cut off small gnocchi of the mixture with an espresso spoon.

THAI CHILE RINGS:

2 TBSP (30 ML) MUSHI SAUCE (→ SEE BASIC RECIPES)
10 GREEN THAI CHILE **RINGS**

Combine the mushi sauce and the chile rings,. Bring to a boil, then vacuumize and infuse for 24 hours.

GARNISH:

FOR EACH PERSON ...
1 LEAF OF HANA-SANSHO FLOWERS

MANNY'S BEEF & ALLIUM

This dish is known as Manny's beef after Manfred "Manny" Höllerschmid, the Austrian butcher from whom we source our beef. He has supplied us for several years, and in addition to his dry-matured beef cuts he also makes a wonderful veal head terrine, plus superb sausages and charcuterie, which we like to eat for our staff lunches.

BEEF:

13 LB (6 KG) SHORT BEEF RIB PIECES
CORNISH SEA SALT
CLARIFIED BUTTER

Generously season the rib pieces with salt, sear in the butter over high heat, then vacuumize. Steam in a Rational Konvektomat for 10 hours at 192 °F (89 °C). Separate the meat from the bones and let cool. Cut into portions of 3½ oz (100 g) each, sear over high heat on both sides, then keep warm in a Lohberger Cook'n'Hold at 156 °F (69 °C).

PEPPER SAUCE:

4½ CUPS (1 L) BEEF TEA
(→ SEE BASIC RECIPES)
7 TBSP (100 ML) MUSHI SAUCE
(→ SEE BASIC RECIPES)
3½ TBSP (50 ML) CHEF SAUCE
(→ SEE BASIC RECIPES)
3 TBSP (21 G) MIXTURE OF WHITE, PINK, AND BLACK PEPPERCORNS, FRESHLY GROUND
1 TBSP (7 G) WILD MADAGASCAR PEPPERS, CRUSHED
3 TBSP (35 G) MUSCOVADO SUGAR
CORNISH SEA SALT
CORNSTARCH

In a saucepan, combine the beef tea, sauces, peppercornss, and sugar, and bring to a boil. Season with salt and thicken with a little cornstarch.

ALLIUM:

FRIED ONIONS
½ CUP (60 G) ALL-PURPOSE FLOUR
¼ CUP PLUS 1 TBSP (60 G) CONFECTIONERS' SUGAR
1 WHITE ONION, PEELED AND THINLY SLICED
FAT FOR DEEP-FRYING
CORNISH SEA SALT

Stir together the flour and the confectioner's sugar. Turn the onion slices in the mixture and deep-fry in fat heated to 365 °F (185 °C). Place onto paper towels, pat dry, and immediately season with salt. Dehydrate in an Excalibur Dehydrator for 3 hours at 140 °F (60 °C). Crush with a mortar and pestle.

SHALLOTS:

10 SHALLOTS, PEELED
2 TBSP (30 ML) GARLIC OIL
(→ SEE BASIC RECIPES)
1 TSP (2 G) GROUND WILD MADAGASCAR PEPPER
CORNISH SEA SALT

Place the shallots in a GN tray lined with aluminum foil. Marinate in the garlic oil and the Madagascar pepper, and generously season with salt. Cover the shallots with another layer of aluminum foil, then cook in the oven for 25 minutes at 320 °F (160 °C).

ONION GEL:

8¾ OZ (250G) WHITE ONIONS, PEELED AND CUT INTO RINGS
1⅔ CUPS (250 G) PEELED AND DICED CELERY ROOT
2 CUPS PLUS 1½ TBSP (500 ML) DUCK BROTH
½ TBSP (4 G) AGAR AGAR POWDER
2 TBSP (30 ML) GEGENBAUER NOBLE-SOUR P.X. VINEGAR

Wrap the onions and the celery root in baking paper and cook in the oven at 356 °F (180 °C) until dark brown.
In a saucepan, bring the duck broth to a boil, add the cooked vegetables, and simmer for 1 hour. Then strain through a cheesecloth. Bring the broth to a boil again and stir in the agar agar powder. Simmer for 5 minutes, then add the vinegar. Transfer to a Thermomix bowl and let cool, then process to a smooth gel. Transfer to a spray bottle.

GARNISH:

FOR EACH PERSON ...
1 LARGE DOT OF GARLIC PUREE
(→ SEE BASIC RECIPES)
2 RED PEARL ONIONS (→ SEE BASIC RECIPES)
3 STEMS THAI CHIVE FLOWERS, BLANCHED AND MARINATED IN A FEW DROPS OF GREEN CHILI SAUCE (→ SEE BASIC RECIPES)
1 TBSP (15 ML) CHIVE OIL
(→ SEE BASIC RECIPES)
A FEW DROPS OF KALAMANSI CITRUS VINEGAR

DONGPO PORK, WATERMELON & MANDARIN ORANGE

The original dish, Dongpo pork belly, is named after the Chinese poet Dong Po. Also known as red-cooked pork, it is especially famous in China as a dish supposedly much favored by Chairman Mao. The recipe below, meanwhile, is my third version of the classic. In order to limit the fattiness of the pork belly, it is served with a refreshing salad of watermelon, mandarin oranges, and green radish, with a bit of galangal for heat.

DONGPO PORK:

3¼ LB (1.5 KG) CURED PORK BELLY
3 QUARTS PLUS ¾ CUP (3 L) WATER
10½ OZ (300 G) PORK BELLY OFFCUTS
14 TBSP (200 ML) RED CHILI SAUCE
(→ SEE BASIC RECIPES)
14 TBSP (200 ML) ROSE'S LEMON CORDIAL
2½ CUPS (120 G) PEELED AND FINELY SLICED GINGER
1 TBSP (15 ML) GROUND STAR ANISE
1 CINNAMON STICK
1 TBSP (15 ML) BONE SUCKIN' HABANERO SAUCE
2 TBSP (30 ML) LOBO ROAST RED PORK SEASONING MIX
½ CUP PLUS 1 TBSP (100 G) MUSCOVADO SUGAR
CORNISH SEA SALT

Vacuumize the pork belly and steam in a Rational CombiMaster for 10 hours at 180 °F (82 °C). Remove the rind and cut the meat into 2 × 1¼ in (5 × 3 cm) pieces.
Put all the remaining ingredients into a saucepan and simmer for 90 minutes, then strain through a fine-mesh strainer. Put the broth into a clean saucepan, bring to a boil again and add the steamed pork belly pieces. Simmer for 15 minutes.

WATERMELON:

30 WATERMELON BALLS, **½ IN (1.5 CM)** DIAMETER
3½ TBSP (50 ML) POMEGRANATE SYRUP

Put the watermelon balls and the syrup into a vacuum bag and vacuumize them. Let infuse for 5 minutes, then remove the watermelon balls.

POMEGRANATE GEL:

1⅔ CUPS (400 ML) WATERMELON JUICE
7 TBSP (100 ML) POMEGRANATE SYRUP
2 TBSP (30 ML) TABASCO GREEN PEPPER SAUCE
1¾ TBSP (7 G) AGAR AGAR POWDER

Put the watermelon juice, pomegranate syrup, and Tabasco into a sauté pan and bring to a boil. Stir in the agar agar powder and simmer for 5 minutes. Transfer to a Thermomix bowl and let cool, then process to a smooth gel. Transfer to a spray bottle.

GARNISH:

FOR EACH PERSON ...
3 SQUARES OF GALANGAL, **¼ × ¼ IN (5 × 5 MM)**
3 MANDARIN ORANGE FILLET HALVES
3 DOTS OF GREEN RADISH PUREE
(→ SEE BASIC RECIPES)
3 STEMS OF WATERCRESS
1 ESPRESSO SPOON (2.5 ML) PARSLEY DRESSING (→ SEE BASIC RECIPES)

首份华人半月刊
扬州
妈妈虽然瘦，但是妈妈胸大
退货

PORK KNUCKLE, DASHI & MUSTARD

Sometimes, weeks go by and I do not create a single new dish. Recently this was the case because I was in the process of devising new products and restaurants, which took up all of my energy. This then generated an internal pressure to bring something extraordinary to the table; yet mostly it doesn't quite work like that. Imagine my pleasure when, after my long period of creative drought, I invented this dish, which I dedicated to my grandmother. As a child, I did not like pork knuckle at all; it was a gray-and-pink monster with a wobbly layer of fat, yellow pea puree, and a cartload of sauerkraut. My version is "Japanized": the fat is paper-thin and crispy, the dashi gel adds flavour, and mustard and ginger add touches of acidity and heat.

PORK KNUCKLE:

1¼ CUPS (300 ML) GARLIC OIL
(→ SEE BASIC RECIPES)
8 TBSP (80 G) CORNISH SEA SALT
8 TBSP (50 G) CARAWAY SEEDS
6 TBSP (55 G) WHITE PEPPERCORNS
10 SUCKLING PIG KNUCKLES
FAT FOR DEEP-FRYING

In a Thermomix, process the garlic oil, salt, caraway seeds, and peppercorns to a paste. Thoroughly rub the paste into the pork knuckles, vacuumize, and let infuse for 6 hours. Steam in a Rational CombiMaster for 10 hours at 180 °F (82 °C). Take the pork knuckles out of the vacuum bags, wash under running hot water, and pat dry with paper towels. Heat the fat in a deep-fryer to 374 °F (190 °C), then deep-fry the pork knuckles in batches for 7 minutes until crispy.

DASHI JELLY:

1⅔ CUPS (400 ML) DASHI
(→ SEE BASIC RECIPES)
10 TBSP (150 ML) ROSE'S LEMON CORDIAL
1 TBSP (7 G) AGAR AGAR POWDER
½ CUP (5 G) EXTRA FINE BONITO FLAKES

In a saucepan, bring the dashi and the lemon cordial to a boil. Stir in the agar agar powder and simmer for 5 minutes, then add the bonito flakes. Pour the jelly onto a baking pan and let cool. Transfer to a Thermomix and process to a smooth mixture, then transfer to a spray bottle.

MUSTARD CREAM:

14 TBSP (200 G) BAUTZ'NER MUSTARD
7 TBSP (100 G) HÄNDLMAIER'S SWEET BAVARIAN MUSTARD
7 TBSP (100 G) JAPANESE MUSTARD

Combine the three types of mustard and transfer to a spray bottle.

GINGER:

14 OZ (400 G) GINGER, UNPEELED
CORNISH SEA SALT
RICE VINEGAR

With a slicer, cut the ginger into wafer-thin slices. Lay the slices flat on baking sheets, sprinkle with salt, and chill. Let degorge for 6 hours. Wash the ginger slices under running lukewarm water, then layer several slices on top of each other in a bowl. Pour the rice vinegar over the ginger slices, cover the bowl with aluminum foil and let the ginger marinate for 30 minutes. Pour off the vinegar. Lay out 3 slices at a time, slightly overlapping, and roll up as a cylinder.

GARNISH:

FOR EACH PERSON ...
3 STEMS ACLLA CRESS®

VEAL, SHISO & JALAPEÑO

This veal composition is a wonderfully summery meat dish. It tastes best of all when partnered with a bottle of the magnificent "Zieregg" Sauvignon Blanc produced by my friend Armin Tement in Styria!

VEAL:

10 VEAL CHEEKS
CLARIFIED BUTTER
CORNISH SEA SALT

Sear the veal cheeks in the butter over high heat. Season with salt, vacuumize, then steam in a Rational CombiMaster for 11 hours at 180 °F (82 °C).

JALAPEÑO SAUCE:

4½ CUPS (1 L) BEEF TEA (→ SEE BASIC RECIPES)
14 TBSP (200 ML) ROSE'S LEMON CORDIAL
2 PICKLED JALAPEÑO PEPPERS, PUREED
2 TBSP (30 ML) JALAPEÑO MARINADE
½ TBSP (4 G) JALAPEÑO PEPPER POWDER
½ CUP PUS 1 TBSP (100 G) MUSCOVADO SUGAR
CORNISH SEA SALT
CORNSTARCH

In a saucepan, bring the beef tea, lemon cordial, pepper puree, marinade, ground pepper, and sugar to a boil, season with the salt and thicken with the cornstarch.

VEAL HEAD DIM SUM:

7 OZ (200 G) HÖLLERSCHMID VEAL HEAD TERRINE, FINELY DICED
4¼ OZ (120 G) POULTRY STUFFING (→ SEE BASIC RECIPES)
6 SHISO LEAVES, CUT INTO PAPER-THIN SLICES
6 TBSP (90 ML) CHEF SAUCE (→ SEE BASIC RECIPES)
2 (7 OZ/200 G) PACKAGES HAPPY BOY WONTON PASTRY

Combine the veal head terrine, poultry stuffing, shiso leaves, and chef sauce. Put 1½ oz (40 g) of the mixture onto each wonton wrapper. Close the wrappers over the filling and steam in a bamboo steamer for 6 minutes.

APPLE AND CELERY BROTH:

14 TBSP (200 ML) PINK LADY APPLE JUICE
10 TBSP (150 ML) CELERY JUICE
2 TRACES OF VITAMIN C POWDER
XANTHAN GUM

Stir the two juices together, season with the vitamin C powder, and thicken lightly with a little xanthan.

CELERY ROOT PASTE:

1 CELERY ROOT, DICED
2 TBSP (30 ML) LEE KUM KEE CHAR SIU SAUCE
2 TBSP (30 ML) HONEY
CORNISH SEA SALT
GROUND WHITE PEPPER
10 TBSP (150 G) JAPANESE MAYONNAISE
½ CUP (120 ML) RED CHILI SAUCE (→ SEE BASIC RECIPES)
2 TBSP (60 ML) CHEF SAUCE (→ SEE BASIC RECIPES)

Combine the celery root dice with the char siu sauce and the honey, then season with salt and pepper. Wrap in aluminum foil, place on a baking sheet and steam in a Rational CombiMaster for 90 minutes at 320 °F (160 °C). Put the mixture onto a wooden board and roughly chop. Stir in the mayonnaise, chili sauce, and chef sauce and let cool. Transfer to a pastry bag and fit the bag with a 1¼ in (3 cm) diameter tip.

APPLE AND CELERY GEL:

4½ TBSP (70 ML) PINK LADY APPLE JUICE
3½ TBSP (50 ML) CELERY JUICE
A TRACE OF VITAMIN C POWDER
1 TSP (1.5 G) AGAR AGAR POWDER

Stir both juices together to combine, flavor with the vitamin C powder, and bring to a boil. Stir in the agar agar powder and simmer for 3 minutes. Pour the mixture into a container and let cool. Process the mixture in a Thermomix until smooth, then transfer to a spray bottle.

GARNISH:

FOR EACH ROLL ...
1 SLICE OF PINK LADY APPLE, **1¾ × 2¾ IN (4.5 × 7 CM)**
1 TSP (5 ML) PINK LADY APPLE DICE
2 DOTS OF JALAPEÑO GEL (→ SEE BASIC RECIPES)
1 FILLETED LIME SEGMENT
¼ SHISO LEAF
3 TBSP (45 ML) FINELY CHOPPED CELERY LEAVES

Roll up the apple slices and fill them with a little celery root paste (SEE LEFT) and the other ingredients. Sprinkle the ends of the rolls with chopped celery leaves.

VENISON, MASSAMAN CURRY & CHINESE ARTICHOKES

This dish is technically by far the most elaborate in this entire book. It takes at least three cooks and two days to prepare it. It is one of those recipes where, even as you read it, you'll decide you'd rather go to a restaurant and enjoy the dish there. And that's what you should do.

VENISON:

10 PIECES OF SADDLE OF VENISON OF
3½ OZ (100 G) EACH, FREED FROM TENDONS
BUTTER FOR FRYING

Wrap the venison saddle pieces tightly in plastic wrap, then in aluminum foil, and cook over a bain-marie for 16 minutes at 142 °F (61 °C). Unwrap the meat and sear on all sides in the butter. Now place the pieces in a Lohberger Cook'n'Hold for 10 minutes at 156 °F (69 °C).

MASSAMAN CURRY SAUCE:

4½ CUPS (1 L) BEEF TEA
(→ SEE BASIC RECIPES)
7 OZ (200 G) VENISON OFFCUTS
14 TBSP (200 ML) MUSHI SAUCE
(→ SEE BASIC RECIPES)
⅓ CUP PLUS 2 TBSP (100 G) SEEDLESS TAMARIND PASTE
¾ CUP (100 G) PALM SUGAR
7 TBSP (100 ML) VEGETABLE OIL
1½ CUPS (400 G) MASSAMAN CURRY PASTE
3 CUPS PLUS 5 TBSP (800 ML) COCONUT MILK
1¼ CUPS (300 ML) PONTHIER COCONUT PUREE
CORNSTARCH
CORNISH SEA SALT

Put the beef tea, venison offcuts, mushi sauce, tamarind paste, and palm sugar into a saucepan and bring to a boil. Simmer for 30 minutes, then strain the broth through a fine-mesh strainer.
Heat the oil in a saucepan, add the massaman paste, and fry over high heat for 3 minutes. Add the strained broth and bring to a boil.
Add the coconut milk and the coconut puree and simmer for 30 minutes. Lightly thicken the sauce with cornstarch and season with the Cornish sea salt.

DIM SUM:

7 OZ (200 G) CHICKEN STUFFING
(→ SEE BASIC RECIPES)
3½ OZ (100 G) VENISON LIVER, PUREED
1¾ OZ (50 G) VENISON HEART, VERY FINELY DICED
1¾ OZ (50 G) VENISON LUNG, PUREED
1½ CUPS (20 G) VERY FINELY CHOPPED THAI BASIL
1 CUP (100 G) CHINESE WALNUTS, CARAMELIZED AND ROUGHLY CHOPPED
7 TBSP (100 G) LEE KUM KEE CHAR SIU SAUCE
2 TBSP (30 ML) THIRTEEN-SPICE POWDER
CORNISH SEA SALT
10 PRESERVED SHIITAKE MUSHROOM HEADS OF **1½ IN (4 CM)** DIAMETER
BUTTER FOR FRYING

Combine all the ingredients apart from the mushrooms and the butter, season with salt. Transfer the stuffing into a pastry bag and pipe it into the mushroom heads. Place the mushrooms, stuffing side up, onto a baking sheet and steam in a Rational CombiMaster for 6 minutes at 180 °F (82 °C). Now fry them in butter, stuffing side down.

SALAD:

PEEL OF 3 JERUSALEM ARTICHOKES
FAT FOR DEEP-FRYING
40 PIECES OF CROSNE
CORNISH SEA SALT

Wash and pat dry the peel. Deep-fry for 70 seconds, place on a Silpat baking mat, and dehydrate in an Excalibur Dehydrator overnight at 131 °F (55 °C). Deep-fry 30 crosne pieces for 2 minutes in fat heated to 356 °F (180 °C). Place onto paper towels, pat dry, and immediately season with salt. Using a truffle shaver, shave the remaining crosne pieces into paper-thin slices and place in iced water.

GARNISH:

FOR EACH PERSON …
3 CASTELFRANCO RADICCHIO LEAVES, CUT OUT AS **¾ IN (2 CM)** DISKS
3 DOTS OF JERUSALEM ARTICHOKE PUREE
(→ SEE BASIC RECIPES)
3 RED PEARL ONIONS (→ SEE BASIC RECIPES)
4 STEMS YARROW
1 TBSP (15 ML) ONION BARBECUE SAUCE
(→ SEE BASIC RECIPES)
2 CHINESE WALNUTS, CARAMELIZED AND QUARTERED

LAMB CHEEKS & YELLOW CURRY

Over time, I've made some good friends in Bangkok, and in addition, my longest-standing colleague and friend Mirco has worked there for years. Mirco was my head chef at the Swissôtel and at Ma Tim Raue in Berlin. He introduced me to Ian Kittichai, and we had a meal at his restaurant, Issaya Siamese Club, which is housed in a beautiful old colonial building. Ian's curries were a knockout, and I've based this Thai-inspired dish on them. Ian is not only a great head chef, he is also a very agile restaurateur, who runs eateries in the United States, Europe, and Asia.

LAMB:

30 LAMB CHEEKS
LEMON OIL (→ SEE BASIC RECIPES)
CORNISH SEA SALT
A HANDFUL OF DRIED CURRY LEAVES

Sear the lamb cheeks on both sides over a high heat in the lemon oil, then generously season with the salt. Place the cheeks with the curry leaves into a vacuum bag and vacuumize.
Steam the lamb cheeks in a Rational CombiMaster for 6 hours at 180°F (82°C). Take out of the vacuum bag, pat dry, and fry again on both sides in the lemon oil.

YELLOW CURRY SAUCE:

4½ CUPS (1 L) CHICKEN BROTH (→ SEE BASIC RECIPES)
7 OZ (200 G) LAMB, DICED
7 TBSP (100 ML) PINEAPPLE JUICE
¾ CUP (100 G) PALM SUGAR
7 TBSP (100 ML) VEGETABLE OIL
1½ CUPS (400 G) YELLOW MASSAMAN CURRY PASTE
1⅔ CUPS (400 ML) COCONUT MILK
7 TBSP (100 ML) PONTHIER COCONUT PUREE
CORNSTARCH
CORNISH SEA SALT

In a saucepan, combine the chicken broth, lamb, pineapple juice, and palm sugar and bring to a boil. Simmer for 30 minutes, then take the saucepan off the heat and let the broth infuse for another 30 minutes. Strain through a fine-mesh strainer.
Heat the oil in a saucepan, add the massaman paste, and fry over high heat for 3 minutes. Pour in the broth and bring to a boil.
Add the coconut milk and the coconut puree and simmer for 30 minutes. Lightly thicken the sauce with a little cornstarch and season to taste with Cornish sea salt.

PINEAPPLE AND PEPPER PUREE:

½ CUP (100 G) PINEAPPLE FLESH
⅓ CUP (50 G) RED BELL PEPPER
1 ESPRESSO SPOON (2.5 ML) VERY FINELY CHOPPED LEMONGRASS

In a Thermomix, combine all the ingredients and process to a puree.

THAI BASIL POWDER:

1 CUP (20 G) THAI BASIL LEAVES

Cover a large plate with plastic wrap. In two batches, place the Thai basil leaves on top and cook in a microwave oven until they are dried. Crush to a powder with a mortar and pestle.

SALAD:

FOR EACH PERSON ...
2 STEMS AFFILA CRESS®
2 STRIPS OF FRESH COCONUT FLESH
2 SLICES OF RIPE BABY BANANA
3 DOTS OF GARLIC PUREE (→ SEE BASIC RECIPES)
2 ROASTED PEANUTS
4 SLICES OF SWEET AND SOUR RED ONIONS (→ SEE BASIC RECIPES)
2 SLICES OF PAPAYA, CUT LENGTHWAYS AND ROLLED UP
1 TBSP (15 ML) MUSHI SAUCE (→ SEE BASIC RECIPES)

MAIALE AL SUGO

Life is unpredictable, and sometimes there is a pleasant surprise. Thus, a few years ago, regulars at the restaurants who had become friends invited me to Sicily. They were so taken by the landscape, the people, and especially the food and the wine that they had bought a house there that was large enough to accommodate guests. I had no particular affinity for Italian cuisine, and even less for Italy's wines, but before long, my friends' enthusiasm rubbed off on me. It is the simplicity of many Italian dishes that I find particularly captivating.

In fact, the following recipe consists only of pork belly braised in tomato sauce. Because of its simplicity you can tell immediately if it has been cooked with love. If you ever travel to Sicily, you really must visit Noto (Café Sicilia), Chiaramonte Gulfi (Ristorante Majore), and Modica (Dolceria Bonajuto & Caffè Adamo), and drink the wines of C&S Biondi, Tenuta delle Terre Nere, and Donnafugata. You won't regret it!

SUGO:

6½ LB (3 KG) CANNED DATTERINO TOMATOES
5 CUPS (900 G) MUSCOVADO SUGAR
3 CUPS PLUS 2 TBSP (750 ML) MUSHI SAUCE (→ SEE BASIC RECIPES)
6 TSP (45 G) GROUND STAR ANISE
6 TBSP (20 G) VERY FINELY DICED GINGER

In a saucepan, combine all the ingredients and bring to a boil. Cover with a lid and simmer for 15 minutes. Transfer to a Thermomix and puree, then return to the saucepan.

MAIALE:

6½ LB (3 KG) CURED PORK BELLY

Cut the pork belly into three pieces of 2 lb 3¼ oz (1 kg) each. Vacuumize the pieces and steam them in a Rational CombiMaster for 10 hours at 180 °F (82 °C). Take the pork out of the bags and remove the rind. Cut the meat into 2 in (5 cm) dice.
Add the pork belly dice to the sugo and simmer everything for 30 minutes.

SWEET 'N' SOUR PORK

If you consider the great classics of Chinese cooking in the West: hot and sour soup, fried noodles with chicken, and especially sweet 'n' sour pork, then you'll understand immediately that this cannot be haute cuisine. They use low-cost ingredients, "thrown together" in a wok, with random aromatics. It has about as much in common with China as a rusty old East German Trabant with the 21st-century automotive industry. Here's a recipe to rehabilitate it: A version of sweet 'n' sour pork that is technically precise and cooked using the very best of ingredients.

PORK BELLY:

4½ LB (2 KG) CURED BELLY OF SUCKLING PIG

Vacuumize the suckling pig pork belly and steam in a Rational CombiMaster for 9 hours at 180 °F (82 °C). Take out of the bag and remove the rind. Vacuumize the belly again and let cool, then cut it into 2 in (5 cm) dice. Place the dice onto a baking sheet, cover with plastic wrap, and cook in the Rational CombiMaster for 20 minutes at 180 °F (82 °C). Glaze with the sweet 'n' sour sauce (SEE RIGHT).

RIND:

7 OZ (200 G) SUCKLING PIG RIND
2 CUPS PLUS 1½ TBSP (500 ML) DASHI
(→ SEE BASIC RECIPES)
6½ CUPS (1.5 L) WATER
FAT FOR DEEP-FRYING

In a sauté pan, combine the rind and the dashi with the water, bring to a boil, and simmer for 90 minutes. Take out the rind and cut into 2 × ⅜ in (5 × 1 cm) strips. Place the strips onto a Silpat baking mat and dehydrate in an Excalibur Dehydrator for 12 hours at 140 °F (60 °C), then deep-fry in fat heated to 392 °F (200 °C). Pat dry with paper towels.

SWEET 'N' SOUR SAUCE:

2 CUPS PLUS 1½ TBSP (500 ML) WATER
1⅔ CUPS (400 ML) RED CHILI SAUCE
(→ SEE BASIC RECIPES)
14 TBSP (200 ML) ROSE'S LEMON CORDIAL
7 TBSP (100 ML) MUSHI SAUCE
(→ SEE BASIC RECIPES)
4 TBSP (60 ML) HOT BANANA KETCHUP
½ CUP (80 G) MUSCOVADO SUGAR
1 TBSP (15 ML) BONE SUCKIN' HABANERO SAUCE
2 TBSP (30 ML) LEE KUM KEE SPARE RIB SAUCE
1 TBSP (15 ML) FIVE-SPICE POWDER
CORNISH SEA SALT
TAPIOCA FLOUR

Put all the ingredients apart from the tapioca flour into a saucepan and bring to a boil. Simmer for 1 hour, then stir in the tapioca flour to make it syrupy.

PINEAPPLE ROLLS:

10 PINEAPPLE SLICES, CUT LENGTHWAYS INTO PAPER-THIN **2¾ × 2½ IN (7 × 6 CM)** STRIPS
1¾ CUPS (300 G) DICED RED BELL PEPPERS
1 CUP PLUS 2 TBSP (200 G) DICED RIPE BEEF TOMATOES
1½ CUPS (80 G) PEELED AND DICED GINGER
VEGETABLE OIL
CORNISH SEA SALT

Place the pineapple strips onto a baking sheet and steam in a Rational CombiMaster for 2 minutes at 180 °F (82 °C). Take out and pat dry. In a wok, fry the peppers, tomatoes, and ginger over high heat in a little vegetable oil. Marinate the vegetables in sweet 'n' sour sauce (SEE LEFT) and season with salt. Place on top of the pineapple slices and roll up.

PINEAPPLE GEL:

4½ CUPS (1 L) PINEAPPLE PUREE
1 ESPRESSO SPOON (2.5 ML) GROUND PONDICHERRY RED PEPPER
½ CUP PLUS 1 TBSP (100 G) MUSCOVADO SUGAR
5 TBSP (80 ML) BROWN RUM
1½ TBSP (12 G) AGAR AGAR POWDER

Combine all the ingredients and bring to a boil, then simmer for 5 minutes. Transfer to a Thermomix bowl and let cool. Process the mixture to a smooth gel, then transfer to a spray bottle.

GARNISH:

FOR EACH PERSON …
3 DOTS OF COCONUT AND CILANTRO CREAM (→ SEE BASIC RECIPES)
3 SLICES OF SWEET AND SOUR RED ONIONS
(→ SEE BASIC RECIPES)
3 STEMS OF GHOA CRESS®

PAPADA SHANGHAI, PAPAYA & CILANTRO

In Shanghai, so it is said, the dishes are always sweet and sour in flavor. After a visit to the city on the Huangpu, my Hong Kong friend, "Chef Tim" of Tim's Kitchen Restaurant, brought me a bottle of sauce, which had been given to him in turn as a present by the head chef of the Li Imperial Cuisine Restaurant. We tried it out in Tim's kitchen, and the aroma was overwhelmingly good. You could taste dried mandarin peel and the sweetness of red fruits, it had the aroma of cinnamon and star anise, and an intense umami note. We had to rush to a photo shoot, and when we got back the bottle was empty. Thanks to our enthusiasm, the cooks succumbed to their curiosity and tried the sauce — and in a flash it had gone. I cooked the sauce below in memory of this event.

PAPADA:

2 LB 3¼ OZ (1 KG) PAPADA (SPANISH-CUT PORK CHEEK)
6 TBSP (90 G) PICKLING SALT
FAT FOR DEEP-FRYING

Sprinkle the papada on all sides with the pickling salt and set aside for 6 hours. Vacuumize the papada and steam in a Rational CombiMaster for 8 hours at 180 °F (82 °C), then hot-smoke for 90 minutes. Cut out slices 2¾ in (7 cm) in diameter from the papada and deep-fry these for 45 seconds in fat heated to 374 °F (190 °C). Glaze the papada with the Shanghai sauce (SEE BELOW).

SHANGHAI SAUCE:

4½ CUPS (1 L) BEEF TEA (→ SEE BASIC RECIPES)
2 CUPS 1½ TBSP (500 ML) RICE WINE
2 CUPS (100 G) PEELED AND THINLY SLICED GINGER
4 SPRING LEEKS, THINLY SLICED
1 CINNAMON STICK
1 TSP (5 ML) GROUND STAR ANISE
1 TSP (5 ML) CASSIA BUDS
1 TSP (5 ML) SESAME OIL
1 TSP (5 ML) BONE SUCKIN' HABANERO SAUCE
2 PIECES OF DRIED MANDARIN ZEST
1 PIECE FRESH ORANGE ZEST
3½ TBSP (50 ML) CHEF SAUCE (→ SEE BASIC RECIPES)
¼ CUP PLUS 1 TSP (50 G) MUSCOVADO SUGAR
CORNSTARCH

Put the beef tea and the rice wine into a sauté pan, bring to a boil and cook to reduce to 4¼ cups (1 liter).
Add all the remaining ingredients apart from the cornstarch to the reduced broth and bring to a boil. Simmer for 30 minutes, take the saucepan off the heat and let infuse for another 30 minutes. Strain the sauce through a cheesecloth, bring to a boil again and lightly thicken with cornstarch

PAPAYA:

2 DOTS OF COCONUT AND CILANTRO CREAM (→ SEE BASIC RECIPES)
20 SLICES OF PAPAYA, CUT LENGTHWAYS AND ROLLED UP
ZEST OF **10** KUMQUATS, WITHOUT THE FLESH AND THE WHITE PITH, QUARTERED
20 STEMS OF GHOA CRESS®

Put the coconut and cilantro cream into the papaya rolls and push in the kumquat zests. Garnish each with a stem of Ghoa Cress®.

GARNISH:

FOR EACH PERSON …
5 SLICES OF SPRING LEEK, SAUTÉED
A PINCH OF SICHUAN PEPPER
2 STEMS GHOA CRESS®

desserts

It was only a few years ago that we fully integrated the patisserie into our kitchen. Before then, we did not follow a clear line in this respect, as we did for the other dishes. We changed that, and decided to focus on fruit,

This development was triggered by my discovery of Japanese fruits. The Japanese, with their typical desire for perfection, breed Cantaloupe melons that boast an aroma and a texture so unreal that they seem to hail from a different world. If you've ever eaten a Japanese peach — as large as a baseball, other-worldly in its juiciness, and scented like a peach perfume — you will never wish to eat anything else.

I once enjoyed strawberries in the fruit section of a department store in Ginza, a bowl of nine fruits wrapped in silk, arranged in a handmade paper carton, and costing ninety dollars. Each individual fruit tasted like an entire field full of ripe, scented strawberries.

Now we are constantly on the lookout for the best, the ripest, and the most delicate of fruits, in order to create refreshingly light desserts from them. We spice our desserts with a piquant acidity and the most diverse varieties of peppers; in addition we use herbs to create a multi-layered aromatic whole.

STRAWBERRIES, THAI BASIL & RHUBARB

The strawberry is the fruit of my childhood. I'll never forget how I picked strawberries in a field but ate more than I kept, and even days later I still smelled of the delicious, ripe fruits. Our creation puts the strawberry at the heart of the dish, using the accompaniments to accentuate its multilayered aromas.

STRAWBERRY MARINADE:

¾ **CUP (100 G)** WILD STRAWBERRIES
¾ **CUP (100 G)** SLICED STRAWBERRIES
⅓ **CUP (75 ML)** ELDERFLOWER SYRUP

In a Thermomix, blend all the ingredients. Marinate the halved strawberries for the garnish in the mixture before serving.

STRAWBERRY GEL:

3¾ CUPS (500 G) SLICED MARA DES BOIS STRAWBERRIES
1¼ TBSP (5 G) AGAR AGAR POWDER

Puree the strawberries and bring to a boil. Stir in the agar agar powder and simmer for 5 minutes. Let cool, transfer into a plastic container, and chill for 4 hours in the fridge. Transfer to a Thermomix and blend to a gel.

SICHUAN PEPPER MERINGUE:

¾ **CUP PLUS 2 TBSP (200 G)** EGG WHITES
3 TBSP (15 G) EGG WHITE POWDER
1½ CUPS (300 G) SUGAR
1 TSP (2 G) LEMON MYRTLE
2 TSP (5 G) GREEN SICHUAN PEPPER, FINELY GROUND

In a mixing bowl, beat the egg whites and the egg white powder to a foam. Gradually add the sugar as you are beating. Fold the lemon myrtle and the Sichuan pepper into the beaten egg whites. The mixture should be stiff. Place ¾ in (2 cm) dots onto a Silpat baking mat and dehydrate in an Excalibur Dehydrator overnight at 131 °F (55 °C).

RHUBARB FOAM:

1¾ CUPS PLUS 2 TBSP (450 G) VAN NAHMEN'S RHUBARB JUICE
2 LEAVES OF GELATIN, SOAKED IN COLD WATER

Heat the rhubarb juice in a saucepan. Squeeze out the gelatin and dissolve in the hot juice. Let the mixture cool and transfer to an iSi flask. Fit the flask with two cream chargers. Chill for 4 hours.

THAI BASIL ICE CREAM:

2½ CUPS (600 ML) LOW-FAT MILK (1.5% FAT)
⅔ **CUP (135 G)** HEAVY CREAM
1 TBSP (15 G) LIME JUICE
2¾ TBSP (75 G) DEXTROSE
⅓ **CUP (75 G)** SUGAR
½ **HEAPED TSP (2.5 G)** GUAR GUM
½ **HEAPED TSP (2.5 G)** LOCUST BEAN GUM
5 CUPS (100 G) THAI BASIL LEAVES
1 CUP (20 G) BASIL LEAVES
¼ **CUP (50 G)** CRÈME FRAÎCHE

Put all the ingredients apart from two basil leaves and the crème fraîche into a Thermomix and process for 10 minutes on Speed 4. Transfer to a container and chill in the fridge overnight. Blanch both types of basil for 5 seconds, then immediately plunge into iced water. Gently squeeze out the leaves. Put the mixture which was chilled overnight, the basil leaves, and the crème fraîche into a Thermomix and process on Speed 10 until smooth. Transfer the mixture to Pacojet beakers and freeze overnight. One hour before serving, pacotize in the Pacojet and freeze again.

GARNISH:

FOR EACH PERSON ...
3 HALVED MARA DES BOIS STRAWBERRIES
6 WILD STRAWBERRIES
6 SHREDS OF THAI BASIL LEAVES
CRÈME FRAÎCHE

QUINCE, MACADAMIA & PASSION FRUIT

I visited the Zotter chocolate factory in Austria and tasted my way through dozens of chocolates when, to my great delight, I suddenly came across a nougat. On my tongue, Zotter's Macadamia Nougat "really phat" is a new benchmark for nougat. Pure sin!

MACADAMIA MOUSSE:

3½ OZ (100 G) MACADAMIA NOUGAT "REALLY PHAT", FINELY CHOPPED
⅔ CUP (150 G) HEAVY CREAM

Put the nougat into a bowl. Bring the cream to a boil and stir into the nougat. Emulsify, and then chill for 2 days. Transfer the mixture into a KitchenAid blender and beat to a mousse.

CARAMEL TUBES:

8¾ OZ (250 G) ISOMALT POWDER
5 OZ (140 G) GLUCOSE POWDER
½ CUP (125 ML) WATER
3 TBSP (40 G) SALTED BUTTER

Put the Isomalt and the glucose powders into a saucepan with the water and cook to a dark caramel. Stir in the butter. Pour onto a Silpat baking mat and let cool. In a Thermomix, process the mixture to dust. Sift the caramel dust onto a Silpat baking mat as 1½ × 3¼ in (4 × 8 cm) rectangles. Place the mat onto a baking sheet and melt the caramel dust under a salamander. Roll the paper-thin caramel sheets around a metal pipe to make a tube. Store in a cool, dry place.

MACADAMIA CRUNCH:

1⅔ CUP (200 G) MACADAMIA NUTS
½ CUP PLUS 1 TBSP (125 G) SUGAR
7 TBSP (125 ML) WATER

Put the nuts and the sugar into a sauté pan with the water and bring to a boil. Continue boiling, stirring constantly, until a caramel forms and sticks to the nuts. Transfer the mixture to a Silpat baking mat and let cool. Roughly crush with a mortar and pestle.

QUINCE AND PASSION FRUIT CHUTNEY:

10½ OZ (300 G) QUINCES, PEELED AND GRATED
FLESH AND SEEDS OF **3** PASSION FRUITS
¼ CUP (50 G) QUINCE CONCENTRATE
¼ CUP (50 G) QUINCE PUREE
2 TBSP (25 G) MUSCOVADO SUGAR
⅓ TBSP (2 G) GROUND STAR ANISE
A PINCH (0.1 G) SAFFRON POWDER
2 TRACES OF GROUND TURMERIC

Put all the ingredients into a saucepan and bring to a boil. Let the mixture cool, then vacuumize it. Cook the chutney in a Rational CombiMaster for 20 minutes at 180 °F (82 °C).

QUINCE GEL:

¼ CUP (50 G) QUINCE CONCENTRATE
¼ CUP (50 G) QUINCE PUREE
10 TBSP (150 G) QUINCE JUICE
2½ TBSP (10 G) AGAR AGAR POWDER
2 TRACES OF GROUND TURMERIC

Put all the ingredients into a sauté pan, bring to a boil, then simmer for 5 minutes. Transfer to a Thermomix bowl and let cool, then process the mixture to a smooth gel. Transfer to a spray bottle.

QUINCE SORBET:

1⅓ CUPS (275 G) QUINCE CONCENTRATE
⅔ CUP (135 G) PASSION FRUIT PUREE
10 TBSP (150 G) WATER
1¼ OZ (37.5 G) GLUCOSE POWDER
2½ TBSP (50 G) HONEY
½ HEAPED TSP (1.3 G) GUAR GUM
½ HEAPED TSP (1.3 G) LOCUST BEAN GUM

Put all the ingredients into a Thermomix and blend for 10 minutes on Speed 6. Transfer the mixture to a Pacojet beaker and chill overnight, then freeze. Pacotize in the Pacojet 1 hour before serving, then freeze again.

GARNISH:

FOR EACH PERSON …
1 STEM PAZTIZZ TOPS®
5 SAFFRON THREADS
A PINCH OF FRESHLY GROUND WILD MADAGASCAR PEPPER

CALPICO, GINGER & GRAPE

Calpico® is a Japanese soft drink that is largely unknown in Europe. A milk-based drink with an unmistakeable flavor, you can find it on the Internet and in well-stocked Asian stores. This dessert was created in homage to André in Singapore. André Chiang and his restaurant have ranked among The World's 50 Best Restaurants for many years, and a visit to his eatery counts as one of the greatest culinary experiences you could have on this planet.
The dessert, consisting of grapes, grape gel, and coriander seeds, was a genuine inspiration. I love the absolute subtlety of the textures, the interplay of sweetness and acidity, and especially the cloud-like Calpico® chiboust cream.

CALPICO® CHIBOUST CREAM:

3 CUPS (750 G) CALPICO®
1 CUP (250 G) YOGURT
12 LEAVES OF GELATIN, SOAKED IN COLD WATER
1¼ CUPS (300 G) EGG WHITE, BEATEN UNTIL STIFF

In a bowl, stir together the Calpico® and the yogurt. Heat one-third of the mixture in a saucepan, add and dissolve the gelatin in the mixture. Return to the bowl and stir well to combine. As soon as the mixture begins to set, immediately fold in the whisked egg white. Transfer the mixture to a deep baking pan lined with baking paper. Let cool for 6 hours, then lift out of the pan and cut into shapes with a cutter.

CALPICO® MERINGUE:

1¼ CUPS (300 G) CALPICO®
6 TBSP (30 G) EGG WHITE POWDER

In a bowl, beat the Calpico® and the egg white powder until the mixture is foamy. Spread the mixture onto a Silpat baking mat and dehydrate overnight in an oven preheated to 131°F (55°C).

GINGER LIQUID:

5 CUPS (500 G) PEELED AND FINELY SLICED GINGER
6½ CUPS (1.5 L) VAN NAHMEN'S RIESLING GRAPE JUICE
XANTHAN GUM

Put the ginger and the grape juice into a saucepan and cook to reduce by half. Lightly thicken the liquid with a few pinches of xanthan.

GRAPE GEL:

3 CUPS PLUS 1½ TBSP (750 ML) VAN NAHMEN'S RIESLING GRAPE JUICE
1 CUP (250 ML) ROSE'S LEMON CORDIAL
2½ TBSP (10 G) AGAR AGAR POWDER

Bring the grape juice and the lemon cordial to a boil. Stir in the agar agar powder and simmer everything for 5 minutes. Transfer to a Thermomix bowl and let cool, then process to a smooth mixture.

GRAPE SORBET:

2¼ CUPS (570 ML) VAN NAHMEN'S RIESLING GRAPE JUICE
14 TBSP (200 ML) ELDERFLOWER SYRUP
3 TBSP (40 ML) ROSE'S LEMON CORDIAL
5¼ OZ (150 G) GLUCOSE POWDER
½ TSP (2 G) GUAR GUM
½ TSP (2 G) LOCUST BEAN GUM

Put all the ingredients into a Thermomix and blend for 10 minutes on Speed 4. Chill overnight, then transfer to a Pacojet beaker and freeze. Pacotize the sorbet in the Pacojet 1 hour before serving and freeze again.

GARNISH:

FOR EACH PERSON ...
7 STEMS OF GHOA CRESS®
6 HALVED THOMPSON SEEDLESS GRAPES
6 QUARTERED THOMPSON SEEDLESS GRAPES

CUCUMBER & PASSION FRUIT

In its original form, this dessert was created by the patissier Jan at my second restaurant, Sra Bua by Tim Raue. I was taken aback by the combination, as I would never have thought of using cucumber and passion fruit together in one dessert. After that, I kept my eyes on Jan, and we transferred him to Restaurant Tim Raue so we could benefit from his creativity and his very distinctive world of flavors.

The Sra Bua by Tim Raue was the first restaurant that I conceived in addition to Restaurant Tim Raue. Based at the Hotel Adlon Kempinkski Berlin, I devised it for the Jagdfeld family's Adlon Holding, opening it in 2008 as the Ma Tim Raue and Uma Restaurant. We left Adlon Holding in the summer of 2010 to set up our own restaurant, but returned in 2013 at the request of the new owners, Hotel Adlon Kempinski, with a casual Asian dining concept. The restaurant kitchen is run by two of my long-standing employees, Daniel Lengsfeld and Marcel Bornschein.

PASSION FRUIT FOAM:

15 TBSP (225 G) YOGURT
⅓ CUP (75 G) SUGAR
12 TBSP (185 G) HEAVY CREAM
⅓ CUP (80 G) PASSION FRUIT PUREE
1 LEAF GELATIN, SOAKED IN COLD WATER

Stir together all the ingredients apart from the gelatin. Squeeze out the gelatin. Heat 4 tablespoons of the mixture, add the gelatin and dissolve, then stir it into the remaining mixture. Transfer to an iSi soda siphon and fit the siphon with two cream chargers.

CUCUMBER SORBET:

1 LB 6 OZ (625 G) CUCUMBER, HALVED AND DESEEDED, BUT WITH PEEL
½ CUP PLUS 1 TBSP (125 G) SUGAR
5¾ OZ (166 G) GLUCOSE POWDER
½ TSP (2 G) GUAR GUM
½ TSP (2 G) LOCUST BEAN GUM
3 TBSP (42 G) PASSION FRUIT PUREE
4 TBSP (62 G) LIME JUICE

In a Thermomix, blend all the ingredients apart from the passion fruit puree and the lime juice for 10 minutes on Speed 4. Transfer to a container and chill in the fridge overnight. Stir the passion fruit puree and the lime juice into the mixture, transfer to a Pacojet beaker, and freeze overnight. Pacotize the sorbet in the Pacojet 1 hour before serving and freeze again.

CUCUMBER JELLY:

2 CUPS (500 G) CUCUMBER JUICE
5¾ OZ (160 ML) ROSE'S LEMON CORDIAL
3 TBSP (40 G) SUGAR
6 LEAVES GELATIN, SOAKED IN COLD WATER

In a saucepan, heat the cucumber juice, lemon cordial, and sugar. Squeeze out the gelatin and dissolve in the liquid. Transfer to blancmange molds and chill for 4 hours, then release the jelly from the molds.

GARNISH:

FOR EACH PERSON ...
1 BORAGE FLOWER

PEAR, CUMIN & FENNEL

Pear and fennel form a part of the category of pre-desserts, which are served after the main course and before the actual dessert. It is the pieces of Montélimar nougat in particular, which make this dish an intense, new taste experience, combining clear notes of aniseed with the sweetness of ripe pears. We bought a special machine to make the slushies, and my chefs now like to use it to mix a watermelon and vodka slushy for themselves at the weekend!

PEAR SLUSHY:

½ CUP PLUS 1 TBSP (125 G) SUGAR
4 TBSP (8 G) JASMINE TEA
2¼ CUPS (500 G) PEAR PUREE

In a saucepan, bring the sugar and 1 cup (250 ml) water to a boil. Add the jasmine tea to the boiling liquid and let infuse for 5 minutes. Strain the tea through a fine-mesh strainer, then stir in the pear puree. Let the mixture cool, then put it into the slushy maker.

CUMIN YOGURT:

¾ CUP PLUS 2 TBSP (200 G) YOGURT
1 TSP (3 G) GROUND CUMIN SEEDS
1 TBSP (20 G) MAPLE SYRUP

Stir all the ingredients to combine.

CHOCOLATE DISKS:

1⅔ CUPS (200 G) CHOPPED DULCEY CHOCOLATE

Melt the chocolate over a bain-marie, then spread it onto chocolate foil. Let cool, then cut out 1¼ in (3 cm) disks using a pre-warmed metal cutter.

GARNISH:

FOR EACH PERSON ...
½ MINI FENNEL, SHAVED INTO PAPER-THIN SLICES AND CHILLED IN ICED WATER
1 ESPRESSO SPOON (2.5 ML) MONTÉLIMAR NOUGAT CHIPS
1 STEM PAZTIZZ TOPS®

BLUEBERRY & FENNEL, CILANTRO

I actually only really like avocados in a prawn cocktail, which is, of course, very "old school", 1980s. In this dessert, however, the avocado forms an excellent balance to the fruit and the acidity, adding volume to the whole dish. The combination of cilantro and blueberries is extraordinary; together with the fennel, it sends the dish in the aromatic direction of a salad. The sweetness of the cream cheese and the freshness of the sorbets unite to create a bittersweet spring dessert.

AVOCADO AND CREAM CHEESE CREAM:

2½ CUPS (300 G) CHOPPED WHITE CHOCOLATE, TEMPERED
8 LEAVES GELATIN, SOAKED IN COLD WATER
1 CUP (250 G) MASCARPONE
¾ CUP PLUS 2 TBSP (200 G) SOUR CREAM
¾ CUP PLUS 2 TBSP (200 G) PHILADELPHIA CREAM CHEESE
2 RIPE AVOCADOS

Melt the chocolate over a bain-marie. Thoroughly squeeze out the gelatin, then dissolve it in the hot chocolate. Add the mascarpone, sour cream, and cream cheese and stir to combine. Peel the avocado, remove the stone, and thoroughly mash the flesh with a fork. Stir it into the cream cheese mixture and transfer the mixture to a bowl. Chill in the fridge for 6 hours. Transfer the cream cheese mixture to a Thermomix and process to a smooth mixture, then transfer to a spray bottle.

CILANTRO COCONUT SORBET:

5 CUPS (100 G) FRESH CILANTRO
1¾ CUPS (400 G) COCONUT PUREE
7 OZ (200 G) SUGAR SYRUP
3 TBSP (40 ML) ROSE'S LEMON CORDIAL
3 TBSP (40 ML) LIME JUICE
1¾ OZ (45 G) BASIC TEXTUR

Briefly blanch the cilantro, then coarsely chop it. Put it into a Thermomix together with the remaining ingredients and blend for 10 minutes on Speed 4. Transfer the mixture to a Pacojet beaker and freeze overnight. Pacotize the sorbet in the Pacojet 1 hour before serving and freeze again.

BLUEBERRY JUICE:

2 CUPS PLUS 2 TBSP (400 G) BLUEBERRIES
2¼ OZ (60 G) SUGAR SYRUP
XANTHAN GUM

Extract the juice from the blueberries, combine with the sugar syrup, then thicken lightly with a little xanthan.

GARNISH:

FOR EACH PERSON ...
5 PIECES OF FRESH COCONUT FLESH
5 BLUEBERRIES
4 PAPER-THIN **SLICES** OF MINI FENNEL
3 STEMS PAZTISS TOPPS®
FRESHLY GRATED LIME ZEST

MANGO, GILOY & LIME

I'm not a friend of vegetables in the patisserie, whereas herbs make for a sensible aromatic complement. In this case, it's really the Thai Nam Dok Mai mango which occupies the foreground. We use a refreshing giloy juice to give some support for its dense sweetness and jungle-like aroma world. The cordifolia is a French lettuce whose fleshy leaves have a bitter-green aroma. We like to use it and highly rate its herbal flavors.

SAFFRON ICE CREAM:

1½ CUPS (375 G) YOGURT
⅓ CUP (85 G) HEAVY CREAM
⅓ CUP (80 G) APRICOT PUREE
¾ CUP (180 G) SUGAR
¼ TSP (0.75 G) SAFFRON POWDER
SCANT ⅓ TSP (1.5 G) GUAR GUM
SCANT ⅓ TSP (1.5 G) LOCUST BEAN GUM

Put all the ingredients into a Thermomix and blend for 10 minutes on Speed 6. Transfer the mixture to a Pacojet beaker and freeze for 24 hours. One hour before serving, pacotize the ice cream in the Pacojet and freeze again

MANGO GEL:

¾ CUP PLUS 2 TBSP (200 G) MANGO PUREE
⅓ CUP PLUS 2 TBSP (100 G) PASSION FRUIT PUREE
1⅓ TBSP (5.5 G) AGAR AGAR POWDER

In a saucepan, bring the mango puree and the passion fruit puree to a boil. Stir in the agar agar powder and simmer for 5 minutes. Let cool, then transfer to a plastic container and chill in the fridge for 4 hours. Transfer to a Thermomix and blend to a paste.

LIME FOAM:

1 CUP (250 G) YOGURT
⅓ CUP (75 G) SUGAR
¾ CUP (185 G) HEAVY CREAM
3½ TBSP (55 ML) LIME JUICE
1 LEAF GELATIN, SOAKED IN COLD WATER

Stir together all the ingredients apart from the gelatin to combine well.
In a saucepan heat 4 tablespoons of the mixture. Squeeze out the gelantine, add to the saucepan and dissolve, then stir the gelatin mixture into the other ingredients.
Transfer to an iSi siphon and fit the siphon with two cream chargers.

LIMEQUAT CHIPS:

8 LIMEQUATS
⅓ CUP (100 G) SUGAR SYRUP

Halve and deseed the limequats, then cut them into slices and transfer to a vacuum bag. Add the sugar syrup, vacuumize, and let infuse for 24 hours. Take the limequat slices out of the syrup and dehydrate in an Excalibur Dehydrator for 48 hours at 131 °F (55 °C).

GILOY LIQUID:

8¾ OZ (250 G) GILOY (TINOSPORA CORDIFOLIA) LEAVES
⅔ CUP (150 G) SUGAR
2 TSP (10 G) LIME JUICE
XANTHAN GUM

Extract the juice from the giloy leaves. Stir in the sugar and the lime juice, check the flavor, and lightly thicken the liquid with 3–4 pinches of xanthan.

GARNISH:

FOR EACH PERSON ...
3 THAI PEPPERCORNS
3 SLICES OF DRIED APRICOT, CUT OUT AS **⅜ IN (1 CM)** DIAMETER DISKS
2 MACADAMIA NUTS, GRATED ON A TRUFFLE SHAVER
4 LENGTHWAYS **STRIPS** OF THAI NAM DOK MAI MANGO

CELERY ROOT, DULCEY & CITRUS FRUITS

Desserts that are based on a combination of vegetables and fruit are a relatively recent development. Here, a mousse of braised celery root with Dulcey chocolate is the velvety-spicy component, with citrus fruits and iced celery creating a fascinating contrast. We only very rarely use liquid nitrogen, but in this case it really does make sense. Liquid nitrogen can be dangerous and must be handled responsibly.

CELERY ROOT PUREE:

1⅔ CUPS (250 G) PEELED AND FINELY DICED CELERY ROOT
7 TBSP (100 ML) MILK
7 TBSP (100 G) HEAVY CREAM
1 TBSP (16 G) MUSCOVADO SUGAR
½ TSP (1.5 G) MALDON SMOKED SEA SALT
1¼ CUPS (150 G) FINELY CHOPPED VALRHONA BLOND DULCEY CHOCOLATE
⅓ CUP (75 G) EGG WHITES
1 CUP (220 G) SUGAR
4 TBSP (60 ML) WATER

Combine the celery root, milk, cream, muscovado sugar, and salt in a saucepan and bring to a boil, then simmer until the liquid becomes glazed. Transfer to a Thermomix and blend to a smooth mixture. Work the chocolate into the mixture while it is still warm.
Beat the egg whites with 2 tablespoons (35 g) sugar until foamy. Combine the remaining sugar and the water in a sauté pan and heat to 237 °F (114 °C), stirring constantly. Add the cooked sugar in a thin stream and beat into the egg white foam. Now fold the mixture into the celery root puree. This puree is freshly made for every service.

MANDARIN JUICE:

2 PINCHES OF XANTHAN GUM
1 CUP (250 G) MANDARIN JUICE

Stir the xanthan gum into the mandarin juice to thicken it lightly.

CHOCOLATE SHEETS:

¾ CUP PLUS 1 TBSP (100 G) CHOPPED VALRHONA BLOND DULCEY CHOCOLATE

Melt the chocolate over a bain-marie. Brush the liquid chocolate onto a piece of chocolate foil, let cool, then shape with a cutter.

CELERY SYRUP & NITROGEN PIECES:

2 CUPS (500 G) CELERY JUICE
¼ CUP (50 G) SUGAR
9 TBSP (130 ML) ROSE'S LEMON CORDIAL
3½ TBSP (50 ML) LIME JUICE
2 TSP (9 G) TABASCO GREEN PEPPER SAUCE
4 PINCHES OF XANTHAN GUM
4½ CUPS (1 L) LIQUID NITROGEN

Stir all the ingredients apart from the xanthan and the liquid nitrogen together to combine. With a hand blender, work in the xanthan to lightly thicken the syrup. Pour half the celery syrup into the liquid nitrogen and freeze for 30 seconds. Smash the frozen syrup into rough pieces. Store in a freezer at -0.4 °F (-18 °C), so that you don't sustain any cold burns.

GARNISH:

FOR EACH PERSON ...
2 LEMON SEGMENT SUPRÊMES, CUT INTO PIECES
2 LIME SEGMENT SUPRÊMES, CUT INTO PIECES
5 SANSHO PEPPERBERRIES
4 GROUND ELDER LEAVES

BANANA, SMOKED BUTTER & YUZU

Personally, I think this is the dessert with the most complex aromatics of my career, but unfortunately it rather polarizes opinion.

BANANA MIXTURE:

3 RIPE BANANAS
1 TBSP (15 ML) VERY FINELY CHOPPED LEMONGRASS
1 TSP (5 ML) VERY FINELY CHOPPED ASIAN LIME LEAVES
JUICE OF ½ LIME

Mash the bananas with a fork, stir in the remaining ingredients.

BANANA JELLY:

2 CUPS (500 ML) BANANA JUICE
1 CUP (250 ML) ROSE'S LEMON CORDIAL
1 CUP (250 ML) WATER
A TRACE OF CITRAS
A TRACE OF GROUND TURMERIC
1½ OZ (40 G) SOSA ELASTIC

Bring the banana juice, lemon cordial, citras, and turmeric powder to a boil with the water. Stir in the elastic. Take the saucepan off the heat and pour the liquid into baking pans so that it is ¾ in (2 mm) deep. Let cool, then cut into 2¾ × 2¾ in (7 × 7 cm) squares.

BANANA YOGURT ICE CREAM:

1½ CUPS (375 G) YOGURT
½ CUP (125 G) HEAVY CREAM
1¾ OZ (50 G) BANANA POWDER
3 TBSP (40 G) LEMON JUICE
1½ CUPS (180 G) CONFECTIONERS' SUGAR
GRATED ZESTS OF **2** LEMONS
1¾ OZ (50 G) BASIC TEXTUR

Blend all the ingredients in a Thermomix for 1 minute on Speed 4. Transfer the mixture to a Pacojet beaker and freeze. Just before serving, briefly pacotize the ice cream in the Pacojet and freeze again.

CHOCOLATE SLICES:

⅔ CUPS (200 G) CHOPPED VALRHONA BLOND DULCEY CHOCOLATE

Melt the chocolate over a bain-marie, then brush onto chocolate foil. Let cool, then cut out ½ in (1.5 cm) diameter disks using a pre-warmed cutter.

CHOCOLATE BLANCMANGE:

1 LEAF GELATIN, SOAKED IN COLD WATER
10½ OZ (100 G) VANILLA BLANCMANGE
(→ SEE BASIC RECIPES)
⅔ CUP (80 G) CHOPPED VALRHONA BLOND DULCEY CHOCOLATE

Thoroughly squeeze out the gelatin, then heat it with a little of the blancmange in a sauté pan until it is completely dissolved. Melt the chocolate over a bain-marie, then stir into the gelatin mixture together with the remaining blancmange. Let cool. Beat the mixture, then transfer to a spray bottle.

BANANA MERINGUE:

⅓ CUP PLUS 2 TBSP (100 G) SUGAR
5 TBSP (25 G) EGG WHITE POWDER
2 TSP (10 ML) FREEZE-DRIED BANANA POWDER
7 TBSP (100 ML) WATER
¼ CUP (30 G) CHOPPED VALRHONA BLOND DULCEY CHOCOLATE

In a KitchenAid, beat the sugar, egg white powder, and banana powder with the water to make a meringue mixture. Transfer to a pastry bag and pipe as thin sticks onto a Silpat baking mat. Dehydrate in an Excalibur Dehydrator overnight. The next day, melt the chocolate over a bain-marie, then dunk the sticks into the liquid chocolate. Store on baking paper.

YUZU SYRUP:

½ CUP (125 ML) YUZU JUICE
7 TBSP (100 ML) ROSE'S LEMON CORDIAL
1 CUP (250 ML) WATER
XANTHAN GUM

Combine the yuzu juice, lemon cordial, and water. Stir in a little xanthan.

SMOKED BUTTER:

2 STICKS PLUS 2 TBSP (1 CUP PLUS 2 TBSP/ 250 G) CLARIFIED BUTTER

Hot-smoke the butter in a smoker one quarter at a time. Serve the butter hot.

GARNISH:

FOR EACH PERSON ...
6 BABY BANANAS, CUT INTO ⅛ **IN (4 MM)** SLICES
CILANTRO CRESS

PRALINÉ MANGO

Since my first visit to Thailand I've been addicted to Nam Dok Mai mangos. Their delicacy can really only be compared to the most heavenly lips that you've ever been allowed to kiss. The mango is velvety-sweet and boasts an incredibly long-lasting aroma. We serve it as a praliné, with salt, sugar, and pepper (as I enjoyed it in Thailand in the street), but in a very un-Thai-like way, we combine it with tarragon. At home I like it best with a little coconut milk and a big scoop of vanilla ice cream.

ITAKUJA TRUFFLES:

7 TBSP (100 G) HEAVY CREAM
⅓ CUP (100 G) SWEETENED CONDENSED MILK
1 OZ (25 G) GLUCOSE POWDER
2½ CUPS (300 G) FINELY CHOPPED ITAKUJA CHOCOLATE
3½ TBSP (50 G) BUTTER
CACAO POWDER

In a sauté pan, bring the cream, condensed milk, and glucose powder to a boil. Let cool to 122 °F (50 °C), then stir in the chocolate, followed by the butter. Transfer the mixture to a bowl and let cool. Using an espresso spoon, cut off small gnocchi shapes, then turn them in cacao powder. Serve cold.

MANGO PÂTE DE FRUITS:

2 CUPS (500 G) NAM DOK MAI MANGO PUREE
1½ OZ (12.5 G) PECTIN
2⅔ CUPS (575 G) SUGAR
3½ OZ (100 G) GLUCOSE SYRUP
2 TBSP (32 G) LIME JUICE
3½ OZ (100 G) MANGO POWDER
7 TBSP (50 G) SICHUAN PEPPER)
5 TBSP (50 G) MALDON SMOKED SEA SALT
½ CUP PLUS 1 TBSP (100 G) MUSCOVADO SUGAR
DRIED LAVENDER FLOWERS

In a Thermomix, blend the mango puree, pectin, and ¼ cup (60 g) of the sugar to a smooth mixture. Put the mixture into a saucepan and bring to a boil. Add the remaining sugar, glucose syrup, and the lime juice and heat everything to 223 °F (106 °C), stirring constantly. Pour the mixture into a rectangular baking pan and let cool. Then cut into cubes, turn the cubes in the mango powder.
In a Thermomix, blend the Sichuan pepper, Maldon sea salt, and muscovado sugar for 1 minute on Speed 10. Sprinkle the mango cubes with a generous pinch of this mixture, then garnish each cube with two lavender flowers.

LIME TARRAGON GEL:

1 CUP (250 G) LIME JUICE
½ CUP PLUS 1 TBSP (125 G) SUGAR
¼ OZ (7.5 G) CITRAS
2¾ TBSP (11 G) AGAR AGAR POWDER
1 CUP (250 ML) WATER
2½ CUPS (50 G) FRESH TARRAGON LEAVES

In a saucepan, bring the lime juice, sugar, citras, agar agar powder, and the water to a boil. Add the tarragon, bring back to a boil and let infuse for 1 hour. Strain the mixture through a fine-mesh strainer, pour it onto a baking pan and let cool. Process in a Thermomix until smooth, then transfer to a spray bottle.

TARRAGON POWDER:

1 CUP (20 G) FRESH TARRAGON LEAVES

Briefly blanch the tarragon leaves, then plunge them into iced water. Carefully squeeze them out. Place the leaves onto a Silpat baking mat and dehydrate in an Excalibur Dehydrator overnight at 131 °F (55 °C). Blend to a powder in a Thermomix.

GARNISH:

FOR EACH PERSON …
1 NAM DOK MAI MANGO, CUT INTO STAR SHAPES
1 LEAF ATSINA® CRESS

RAMBUTAN, RASPBERRY & PALM SEEDS

Originally I created this aromatic union as a dessert to accompany Krug Rosé champagne. This champagne is superbly full-bodied; it boasts the noble structure of a pinot noir, but also a certain severity, since it is characterized by modest fruitiness and hardly any sweet notes. Visually, I define it as a strict grandmother of the English kind, who does not show her warmth until she is surrounded by her sugary sweet grandchildren. Here, the place of the grandchildren is taken by the rambutan and the raspberries.

RAMBUTAN, PALM SEEDS & ASIAN LIME LEAF SALAD:

20 RAMBUTANS
40 PALM SEEDS IN SYRUP
4 ASIAN LIME LEAVES
JUICE OF **2** LIMES
15 ML (1 TBSP) ROSEWATER

Halve the rambutans. Separate the flesh from the stone and cut the flesh into strips. Cut the palm seeds into strips. Cut the Asian lime leaves first into very thin strips, then into very fine dice. Combine with the lime juice and the rose water. Marinate the rambutan and palm seed strips in the liquid.

RAMBUTAN PÂTE DE FRUITS:

2¾ CUPS (500 G) RAMBUTAN FLESH
2 TBSP (12 G) PECTIN
2¾ CUPS PLUS 2 TBSP (625 G) SUGAR
2½ OZ (67.5 G) GLUCOSE
1 TBSP (15 G) LIME JUICE

In a saucepan, bring the rambutan flesh to a boil with the pectin and ⅓ cup (75 g) of the sugar. Add the remaining sugar, the glucose, and lime juice, then heat to 225 °F (107 °C), stirring constantly. Transfer to a rectangular baking pan and let cool.

YOGURT ICE CREAM:

1½ CUPS (375 G) YOGURT
½ CUP (125 G) HEAVY CREAM
3 TBSP (40 G) LIME JUICE
GRATED ZEST OF **2** LIMES
1½ CUPS (180 G) CONFECTIONERS' SUGAR
1¾ OZ (50 G) BASIC TEXTUR

In a Thermomix, combine all the ingredients and blend for 10 minutes on Speed 4. Transfer to a Pacojet beaker and freeze overnight. Pacotize in the Pacojet 1 hour before serving and freeze again.

ASIAN LIME LEAF FOAM:

3½ TBSP (50 ML) SUGAR SYRUP
3½ TBSP (50 ML) ROSE'S LEMON CORDIAL
3½ TBSP (50 ML) HEAVY CREAM
4 ASIAN LIME LEAVES

Blend all the ingredients in a Thermomix for 1 minute on Speed 8. Then vacuumize and let infuse for 1 hour. Strain through a fine-mesh strainer and transfer to an iSi soda siphon. Fit the siphon with two cream chargers.

ROSE MARSHMALLOW:

1 CUP (250 G) RASPBERRY JUICE
1 TBSP (12 G) ROSEWATER
2 TBSP (25 G) SUGAR
2 LEAVES OF GELATIN, SOAKED IN COLD WATER

In a sauté pan, combine and heat the raspberry juice, rosewater, and sugar. Squeeze out the gelatin, add and dissolve. Transfer the mixture to a KitchenAid mixing bowl and slowly beat until foamy. Fit a pastry bag with a plain tip, transfer the mixture to the bag, then pipe as long strings onto a Silpat baking mat. Let chill in the fridge for 3 hours.

GARNISH:

FOR EACH PERSON ...
A TRACE OF RASPBERRY POWDER
3 RASPBERRIES
3 TIPS OF FRESH LEMON VERBENA
5 FRESH ROSE PETALS
8 DOTS OF CRÈME FRAÎCHE

PRALINÉ KUMQUAT

At the end of an evening meal we finish with what we call pralinés. These are served as a three-part course, consisting of chocolate truffles, pâte de fruits, and a fresh fruit component, all presented in a Japanese bento box.

KUMQUAT TRUFFLES:

¾ CUP PLUS 2 TBSP (200 G) HEAVY CREAM
2½ TBSP (38 G) BUTTER
2½ CUPS (400 G) MILK CHOCOLATE CALLETS
⅔ CUP (100 G) WHITE CHOCOLATE CALLETS
2 TBSP (25 G) KUMQUAT OIL
CACAO POWDER

In a saucepan, heat the cream and the butter. Put the callets into a bowl, pour over the cream and butter mixture, and stir everything to combine. Now stir in the oil. Transfer the mixture to a container and let cool. Using an espresso spoon, cut off small gnocchi shapes, then turn them in the cacao powder.

KUMQUAT CALAMANSI PÂTE DE FRUITS:

¾ CUP PLUS 2 TBSP (200 G) KUMQUAT PUREE
¾ CUP PLUS 2 TBSP (200 G) CALAMANSI (CALAMONDIN) PUREE
10 TBSP (150 ML) LIME JUICE
¾ OZ (25 G) PECTIN
2¾ CUPS PLUS 2 TBSP (625 G) SUGAR
1 OZ (30 G) CITRAS
2 TBSP (25 ML) WATER
4 TSP (2 G) SAFFRON THREADS
3½ OZ (100 G) KUMQUAT POWDER

In a saucepan, stir to combine the kumquat puree and the Calamansi puree with 7 tablespoons (100 ml) of the lime juice, the pectin, ¼ cup (50 g) of the sugar, and the citras. Bring to a boil. Add the remaining lime juice, sugar, and the water. Heat the mixture to 225°F (107°C), stirring constantly. Now stir the saffron threads into the hot mixture, then pour into a ¾-in (2-cm)-high metal frame. Let cool, then cut into ¾ × ¾ in (2 × 2 cm) cubes. Turn the cubes in the kumquat powder. Store in a cool place.

ICED KUMQUATS:

½ CUP (80 G) KUMQUAT FLESH, DESEEDED
5 TBSP (80 ML) POMELO JUICE
1 TSP (5 G) SUGAR
1 TBSP (15 ML) LIME JUICE
1 TBSP (15 ML) ROSE'S LEMON CORDIAL
A PINCH (0.5 G) GUAR GUM
A PINCH (0.5 G) LOCUST BEAN GUM
40 KUMQUATS, HALVED, HOLLOWED OUT AND FROZEN
20 DOTS OF HONEY
20 STEMS GHOA CRESS®

Put all the ingredients apart from the halved kumquats, honey, and cress into a Thermomix and blend for 10 minutes on Speed 4. Let cool overnight. Transfer into a Pacojet beaker and freeze. Pacotize the sorbet in a Pacojet 1 hour before serving, then freeze again.
Transfer the sorbet into the kumquat shells, smooth the top, glaze with the honey, and garnish with the cress.

basic recipes

1

BEEF TEA

3¼ LB (1.5 KG) BEEF, WAGYU BEEF RIB IF POSSIBLE
3 QUARTS PLUS 1 CUP (3 L) WATER
1¼ CUPS (300 ML) RICE WINE
1⅔ CUP (300 G) MUSCOVADO SUGAR
1 CUP PLUS 2 TSP (250 ML) MUSHI SAUCE (→ SEE NO. 19)
⅔ CUP (100 G) PEELED AND FINELY DICED CARROTS
⅔ CUP (100 G) PEELED AND FINELY DICED ONIONS
1 CUP (100 G) FINELY DICED CELERY
2 TBSP LEE KUM KEE CHAR SIU SAUCE
1 TBSP BONE SUCKIN' HABANERO SAUCE
CORNISH SEA SALT
10½ OZ (300 G) GROUND BEEF
¾ CUP PLUS 1 TBSP (200 G) EGG WHITE

Put all the ingredients apart from the ground beef and the egg white into a large saucepan; simmer for 40 minutes. Strain through a fine-mesh strainer and let the liquid cool completely. Add the ground beef and the egg white to the saucepan and stir to combine. Slowly bring the beef tea to a boil, simmer for 5 minutes. Take off the heat and let infuse for 30 minutes. Strain through a cheesecloth.

2

CHEF SAUCE

7½ CUPS (1.8 L) SEKIGAHARA TAMARI SOY SAUCE
7½ CUPS (1.8 L) DASHI (→ SEE NO. 6)
32 CUPS (800 G) FRESH LOVAGE
1 LB 1½ OZ (500 G) DRIED MUSHROOMS (PORCINI, BUTTON MUSHROOMS, CHANTERELLES)
2½ TBSP (25 G) FINELY CHOPPED RED THAI CHILES

Combine all the ingredients in a saucepan and bring to a boil. Transfer to a large container and let cool. Cover with a lid and place in the fridge to marinate for 24 hours. Strain the sauce through a cheesecloth.

3

CHICKEN BROTH

3 LB (1.5 KG) CHICKEN LEGS
3 QUARTS PLUS 1 CUP (3 L) WATER
2½ CUPS (600 ML) ROSE'S LEMON CORDIAL
14 TBSP (200 ML) ELDERFLOWER SYRUP
14 TBSP (200 ML) GREEN CHILI SAUCE (→ SEE NO. 13)
1 CUP (100 G) FINELY DICED CELERY
⅔ CUP (100 G) PEELED AND CHOPPED CELERY ROOT
CORNISH SEA SALT

Put all the ingredients into a saucepan, bring to a boil, and simmer for 30 minutes. Strain the broth through a cheesecloth and let cool.

4

CHIVE OIL

A BUNCH OF CHIVES, ROUGHLY CHOPPED
4½ CUPS (1 L) VEGETABLE OIL

Blend the chives and the oil together in a Thermomix for 5 minutes on Speed 10. Transfer to a vacuum bag, vacuumize, and let infuse for 24 hours. Strain through a fine-mesh strainer. Store the oil in a cool place

5

COCONUT & CILANTRO CREAM

2 CUPS (500 G) PONTHIER COCONUT PUREE
CORNSTARCH
30 CUPS (750 G) CILANTRO LEAVES
5 TBSP (80 ML) TABASCO GREEN PEPPER SAUCE
7 TBSP (100 ML) GREEN CHILI SAUCE (→ SEE NO. 13)
1 TBSP (15 ML) CORNISH SEA SALT

In a sauté pan, bring the puree to the boil and add cornstarch until it has a blancmange-like consistency. Blanch the cilantro in salted water, then immediately plunge it into iced water. Finely chop the leaves and add to the coconut puree. Stir in the Tabasco and the chili sauce and season with salt. Pour the cream into 2 Pacojet beakers and freeze overnight. The next day, pacotize the cream and pour into spray bottles.

6

DASHI

4½ CUPS (1 L) CHICKEN BROTH (→ SEE NO. 3)
3½ OZ (100 G) KOMBU SEAWEED
2 CUPS (20 G) KATSUOBUSHI (BONITO FLAKES)
⅔ CUP (100 G) PEELED AND CHOPPED CELERY ROOT
1 BAY LEAF

Combine all the ingredients in a saucepan, bring to a boil and simmer for 15 minutes. Then simmer for 1 hour over a medium heat. Strain the liquid through a cheesecloth.

7

DUCK BROTH

4½ LB (2 KG) DUCK LEGS
½ OZ (15 G) STAR ANISE
⅓ OZ (12 G) CINNAMON STICKS
2 TBSP (20 G) CORNISH SEA SALT
1½ TBSP (20 ML) CHEF SAUCE (→ SEE NO. 2)
1½ TBSP (20 ML) SEKIGAHARA TAMARI SOY SAUCE
⅔ CUP (180 G) LEE KUM KEE CHAR SIU SAUCE
1¼ CUPS (300 ML) RICE WINE
1¼ CUPS (300 ML) MUSHI SAUCE (→ SEE NO. 19)
½ CUP (100 G) MUSCOVADO SUGAR
3 QUARTS PLUS 3 CUPS (3.5 L) WATER
1⅔ CUPS (400 ML) EGG WHITE
4 CUPS (600 G) ICE CUBES

Put all the ingredients apart from the egg white and the ice cubes into a very large saucepan. Bring to a boil and simmer for 3 hours, then pass through a fine-mesh strainer. In a bowl, combine the egg white and the ice cubes, then add to the hot broth. Bring back to a boil and simmer for 10 minutes. Strain through a cheesecloth.

8

GARLIC CHIPS

10 LARGE GARLIC CLOVES, PEELED
FAT FOR DEEP-FRYING

Cut the garlic into wafer-thin (about 1 mm) slices, then deep-fry them in fat heated to 266 °F (130 °C) until lightly browned. Place onto paper towels and pat dry. Dehydrate overnight at 131 °F (55 °C) in an Excalibur Dehydrator.

9

GARLIC OIL

1 CUP PLUS 1 TBSP (250 ML) VEGETABLE OIL
3½ OZ (100 G) GARLIC, PEELED

Blend the oil and the garlic in a Thermomix for 2 minutes on Speed 10. Transfer the mixture to a vacuum bag and vacuumize. Steam the oil and garlic in a Rational CombiMaster for 4 hours at 180 °F (82 °C).

10

GARLIC PUREE

6⅔ CUPS (1 KG) PEELED AND FINELY DICED WHITE ONIONS
¾ CUP (100 G) PEELED AND FINELY SLICED GARLIC
1 STICK (100 G) BUTTER
14 TBSP (200 ML) MILK
3½ TBSP (50 ML) CREAM
5 TBSP (80 ML) MUSHI SAUCE (→ SEE NO. 19)
CORNISH SEA SALT
GROUND WHITE PEPPER

Sauté the onions and the garlic in the butter. Add the milk, cream, and mushi sauce, stir and simmer for 1 hour. Put the mixture into a Thermomix and process to a smooth puree. Season with salt and pepper.

11

GINGER JELLY

3 CUPS (700 ML) ROSE'S LEMON CORDIAL
1¼ CUPS (300 ML) WATER
1¼ CUPS (300 ML) SUSHI GINGER JUICE (→ SEE NO. 33)
5 CUPS (500 G) PEELED AND FINELY SLICED FRESH GINGER
10½ OZ (300 G) GARI (SUSHI GINGER)
1 STALK LEMONGRASS, VERY FINELY CHOPPED
10 ASIAN LIME LEAVES
3 TBSP (12 G) AGAR AGAR POWDER

Put all the ingredients apart from the agar agar powder into a saucepan and bring to a boil, simmer for 15 minutes. Strain through a fine-mesh strainer into a clean saucepan, bring back to a boil and stir in the agar agar powder. Simmer for 5 minutes. Pour the jelly into a deep baking pan and let cool. Transfer to a Thermomix and process until smooth.

12

GREEN CHILI GEL

14 TBSP (200 ML) GREEN CHILI SAUCE (→ SEE NO. 13)
14 TBSP (200 ML) MUSHI SAUCE (→ SEE NO. 19)
¼ CUP (50 G) SUGAR
4 GREEN THAI CHILES, DESEEDED AND FINELY CHOPPED
XANTHAN GUM

Put all the ingredients apart from the xanthan into a sauté pan, bring to a boil and simmer for 15 minutes. Take off the heat and let cool. Put the liquid into a Thermomix and process for 3 minutes on Speed 10. Add a little xanthan until the gel is syrupy.

13

GREEN CHILI SAUCE

8 CUPS (2 LITER) SUGAR SYRUP
½ CUP (75 G) GARLIC, PEELED AND FINELY CHOPPED
1¼ CUPS (220 G) DESEEDED AND FINELY CHOPPED GREEN CHILES
¾ CUP (100 G) PICKLED JALAPEÑO PEPPERS, FINELY CHOPPED
3 TBSP (45 ML) VINEGAR ESSENCE
3 TBSP (30 G) CORNISH SEA SALT
1⅔ CUPS (400 ML) WATER
1⅓ CUPS PLUS 1 TBSP (180 G) CORNSTARCH

Put all the ingredients apart from the cornstarch into a saucepan and bring to a boil. Stir the cornstarch into the boiling sauce and simmer for 5 minutes. Take the sauce off the stove and let cool. Mix for 3 minutes with a hand blender.

14

GREEN RADISH PUREE

6⅔ CUPS (1 KG) DICED GREEN DAIKON
4 TBSP (60 ML) RICE VINEGAR
1½ TBSP (15 G) CORNISH SEA SALT
2 TBSP (30 G) SUGAR
½ ESPRESSO SPOON (2.5 ML) GROUND WHITE PEPPER

Put all ingredients into a Thermomix and blend for 1 minute at Speed 3. Transfer the puree to a strainer and allow the liquid to drain away. Put the mixture into a sauté pan, cover with a lid and sauté over low heat until soft. Return to the Thermomix and blend for 1 minute on Speed 4. Season the puree again to taste with a little rice vinegar, salt, sugar, and white pepper.

15

JALAPEÑO JELLY

7⅔ CUPS (1 KG) GOYA JALAPEÑO PEPPERS
14 TBSP (200 ML) JALAPEÑO MARINADE
3½ TBSP (50 ML) RICE VINEGAR
XANTHAN GUM

Put all the ingredients apart from the xanthan into a Thermomix and process until smooth. Add a little xanthan until the mixture has a jelly-like consistency. Transfer into a spray bottle.

16

JERUSALEM ARTICHOKE PUREE

5⅓ CUPS (800 G) JERUSALEM ARTICHOKES, PEELED AND SLICED
2 TBSP (25 G) BUTTER
CORNISH SEA SALT
WHITE PEPPER
7 TBSP (100 ML) MILK
XANTHAN GUM

Sauté the Jerusalem artichokes in the butter, then season with salt and pepper. Add the milk, cover with a lid, and sauté for 15 minutes until soft. Strain off the liquid. Put the Jerusalem artichokes into a Thermomix and process to a smooth puree. Thicken the puree with a little xanthan gum, and season again with salt and pepper.

17

LEEK AND GINGER PUREE

5 LBS 8 OZ (2.5 KG) TRIMMED AND FINELY SLICED LEEKS
CORNISH SEA SALT
12⅓ OZ (350 G) PEELED AND FINELY CHOPPED GINGER
2 STALKS LEMONGRASS, VERY FINELY CHOPPED
6½ CUPS (1.5 L) WATER
2½ TBSP (10 G) AGAR AGAR POWDER
TABASCO GREEN PEPPER SAUCE

Cook the leeks in salted water until soft, then gently squeeze out. Put them into a Pacojet beaker and let freeze completely overnight. Pacotize the frozen leeks, then freeze and pacotize again. Repeat the process three times, until the mixture has turned into a leek powder.
Put the ginger, lemongrass and water into a saucepan and cook for 45 minutes. Strain the liquid and bring back to a boil. Stir the agar agar powder into the boiling liquid, then let simmer for 5 minutes. Pour the mixture onto a baking pan and let cool. Put it into a Thermomix and process to a smooth gel. Stir the leek powder into the gel. Season with Tabasco green pepper sauce.

18

LEMON OIL

8 CUPS (2 L) VEGETABLE OIL
4 CUPS (400 G) FINE STRIPS OF UNTREATED LEMON ZEST

Vacuumize together the oil and the lemon zest. Steam for 2 hours at 180 °F (82 °C) in a Rational CombiMaster, then let cool in iced water. Repeat this process four times. Leave in the vacuum bag for 1 week to infuse, then strain through a cheesecloth.

19

MUSHI SAUCE

3 QUARTS PLUS 1 CUP (3 L) SUGAR SYRUP
6¾ CUPS (1.6 L) MEGACHEF PREMIUM FISH SAUCE
1½ CUPS (200 G) PEELED AND FINELY CHOPPED GARLIC
2¾ CUPS (500 G) DESEEDED AND FINELY CHOPPED RED CHILES
7 TBSP (100 ML) VINEGAR ESSENCE
5 TBSP (50 G) CORNISH SEA SALT
3¾ CUPS (900 ML) WATER

In a saucepan, bring all the ingredients to a boil. Take the sauce off the stove and let cool. Puree with a hand blender for 3 minutes.

20

ONION BARBECUE SAUCE

6⅔ CUPS (1 KG) PEELED AND DICED WHITE ONIONS
6⅔ CUPS (1 KG) PEELED AND FINELY DICED CELERY ROOT
8 CUPS (2 L) DUCK BROTH (→ SEE NO. 7)
4½ CUPS (1 L) DASHI (→ SEE NO. 6)
4½ CUPS (1 L) MUSHI SAUCE (→ SEE NO. 19)
5½ CUPS (1 KG) MUSCOVADO SUGAR
1 CUP PLUS 2 TBSP (350 G) LEE KUM KEE CHAR SIU SAUCE
¾ CUP PLUS 2 TBSP (200 G) TOMATO KETCHUP
⅓ CUP (80 G) TOMATO PASTE
2 TBSP (30 ML) PICANTE PIMENTÓN
2 TBSP (30 ML) CHEF SAUCE (→ SEE NO. 2)
XANTHAN GUM

Wrap the onions and celery root in aluminum foil and cook on a charcoal broiler. Put all the remaining ingredients apart from the xanthan into a saucepan, bring to a boil and simmer for 15 minutes. Process the onions, the celery root, and the sauce in batches in a Thermomix. Let cool. Thicken the sauce with the xanthan to a syrupy consistency.

21

ORANGE OIL

8 CUPS (2 L) VEGETABLE OIL
4 CUPS (400 G) THIN STRIPS OF PEEL FROM UNTREATED ORANGES

Put both ingredients into a vacuum bag and vacuumize. Steam in a Rational CombiMaster at 180 °F (82 °C) for 2 hours, then let cool in iced water. Repeat the process four times. Let infuse for 1 week in the vacuum bag, then strain through a cheesecloth.

22

PARSLEY CREAM

PARSLEY ROOT PUREE
14¼ OZ (400 G) PARSLEY ROOTS, FINELY SLICED
⅔ CUP (100 G) PEELED AND FINELY DICED WHITE ONION
3½ TBSP (50 G) BUTTER
14 TBSP (200 ML) MILK
7 TBSP (100 ML) WATER

Lightly sauté the parsley roots and the onion in the butter without coloring them. Add the milk and the water, cover with a lid, then simmer for 1 hour. Strain off the liquid, put the vegetables into a Thermomix and process to a smooth puree.

PARSLEY POWDER
13⅓ CUPS (200 G) PARSLEY
CORNISH SEA SALT

Cook the parsley in salted water until softened, then plunge into iced water and gently squeeze out. Put it into a Pacojet beaker and freeze overnight. Pacotize and freeze again. Repeat the process three times until you have a parsley powder.

⅓ CUP PLUS 2 TBSP (100 G) CRÈME FRAÎCHE
3½ TBSP (50 G) JAPANESE MAYONNAISE
3½ TBSP (50 ML) GREEN CHILI GEL (→ SEE NO. 12)
CORNISH SEA SALT

In a bowl, stir together the parsley root puree, the parsley powder, and the remaining ingredients. Season with salt and pour into a spray bottle.

23

PARSLEY DRESSING

6⅔ CUP (100 G) PARSLEY
2½ TBSP (40 G) SUGAR
1 TBSP (15 ML) MUSTARD
7 TBSP (100 ML) DASHI (→ SEE NO. 6)
7 TBSP (100 ML) RICE VINEGAR
3½ TBSP (50 ML) YUZU JUICE
2 TBSP (30 ML) LEMON OIL (→ SEE NO. 18)
4½ TBSP (70 ML) VEGETABLE OIL

Cut the parsley into very thin strips. Put it into a Thermomix with the sugar, mustard, dashi, rice vinegar, and yuzu juice and blend for 5 minutes on Speed 6. Combine the two oils and blend into the parsley mixture on Speed 3. Strain the dressing through a fine-mesh strainer.

24

PARSLEY ROOT PUREE

2 LB 31/4 OZ (1 KG) PEELED AND FINELY DICED PARSLEY ROOTS
2 STICKS PLUS 1½ TBSP (1 CUP PLUS 1½ TBSP/250 G) BUTTER
7 TBSP (100 ML) LEMON OIL (→ SEE NO. 18)
4½ CUPS (1 L) MILK
2 CUPS PLUS 1½ TBSP (500 G) HEAVY CREAM
2 CUPS PLUS 1½ TBSP (500 ML) WATER
CORNISH SEA SALT
GREEN CHILI SAUCE (→ SEE NO. 13)
AGAVE NECTAR

In a saucepan, sauté the parsley root dice in the butter and the lemon oil, without letting them discolor. Add the milk, cream, and water, and bring to a boil. Let everything simmer until all the liquid has disappeared. Put the mixture into a Thermomix and process to a smooth puree. Season the puree with salt, chilli sauce, and agave nectar.

25

PLUM SAUCE FOR PEKING DUCK

3 CUPS PLUS 2 TBSP (750 ML) MARSALA
1 CUP PLUS 1½ TBSP (300 G) LEE KUM KEE CHAR SIU SAUCE
1¾ CUPS (400 G) PLUM PUREE
¾ CUP PLUS 1 TBSP (150 G) MUSCOVADO SUGAR
1 TBSP (15 ML) GROUND WHITE PEPPER
XANTHAN GUM

In a saucepan, combine all the ingredients apart from the xanthan and bring to a boil, then simmer for 15 minutes. Take off the stove and let cool. Add a little xanthan until the mixture has a syrupy consistency.

26

POULTRY STUFFING

3½ OZ (100 G) TURKEY BREAST
3½ OZ (100 G) CHICKEN MEAT
3½ OZ (100 G) BACON
14 TBSP (200 G) HEAVY CREAM
2 LARGE EGGS

Skin the turkey breast, remove fat and sinews, then finely dice the breast. Grind the chicken meat and the bacon twice, using the finest cutting blade. Combine the turkey, chicken, and bacon with the cream and the eggs, and transfer to a Pacojet beaker. Pacotize four times.

27

RED CHILI COMPOTE

4½ CUPS (**1 L**) MUSHI SAUCE, STRAINED (→ SEE NO. 19),
3¼ CUPS (**250 G**) SLICED DRIED RED CHILES, CUT INTO RINGS
1¼ TBSP (**5 G**) AGAR AGAR POWDER

In a saucepan, bring the mushi sauce to a boil with the chile rings. Stir in the agar agar powder and simmer for 5 minutes. Pour the mixture into a baking pan and let cool. Process to a smooth mixture in a Thermomix, then pour into a spray bottle.

28

RED CHILI SAUCE

8 CUPS (**2 L**) SUGAR SYRUP
⅔ CUP (**80 G**) GARLIC, PEELED AND FINELY CHOPPED
1¼ CUPS (**220 G**) FINELY CHOPPED RED CHILES
3 TBSP (**40 ML**) VINEGAR ESSENCE
1⅔ CUPS (**400 ML**) WATER
3 TBSP (**30 G**) CORNISH SEA SALT
1⅓ CUPS PLUS 1 TBSP (**180 G**) CORNSTARCH

Combine all the ingredients apart from the cornstarch and bring to a boil. Stir the cornstarch into the boiling sauce and simmer for 5 minutes. Take the sauce off the heat and let cool, then puree with a hand blender for 3 minutes.

29

RED PEARL ONIONS

6¼ CUPS (**1 KG**) PEARL ONIONS, PEELED
14 TBSP (**200 ML**) RASPBERRY VINEGAR
14 TBSP (**200 ML**) PORT
6 TBSP (**90 ML**) BEET POWDER
⅔ CUP (**150 G**) SUGAR

In a saucepan, combine the raspberry vinegar, port, beet powder, and sugar, then bring to a boil. Add the pearl onions and simmer for 10 minutes. Take off the heat and let cool. Vacuumize and let infuse for 24 hours.

30

SHELLFISH MAYONNAISE

7 TBSP (**100 ML**) JAPANESE MAYONNAISE
4 TBSP (**60 ML**) ORANGE OIL (→ SEE NO. 21)
2 TBSP (**30 ML**) LOBSTER CORAL
2 TBSP (**30 ML**) LANGOUSTINE HEADS, WITHOUT SHELLS
1 TBSP (**15 ML**) HOT BANANA SAUCE
1 TBSP (**15 ML**) BONE SUCKIN' HABANERO SAUCE

Blend all the ingredients in a Thermomix.

31

SHELLFISH BROTH

2 LB 3¼ OZ (**1 KG**) SHELLFISH CARCASSES
8 CUPS (**2 L**) WATER
1¼ CUPS (**300 ML**) ROSE'S LEMON CORDIAL
14 TBSP (**200 ML**) RED CHILI SAUCE (→ SEE NO. 28)
¾ CUP PLUS 1 TBSP (**150 G**) MUSCOVADO SUGAR
⅔ CUP (**100 G**) FINELY DICED RED BELL PEPPER
½ CUP (**100 G**) FINELY DICED RIPE TOMATOES
⅔ CUP (**100 G**) FINELY DICED CARROTS
CORNISH SEA SALT
1¼ CUPS (**300 G**) EGG WHITE

In a saucepan, bring all the ingredients apart from the egg white to the boil, then simmer for 30 minutes. Strain the broth through a cheesecloth and let cool. Stir the egg white into the cold broth, then slowly bring the broth back to a boil. Take off the heat and let infuse for 10 minutes. Strain again through a cheesecloth.

32

SMOKED OIL

4½ CUPS (**1 L**) VEGETABLE OIL

Hot-smoke the oil in a smoker. Repeat the process four times.

33

SUSHI GINGER JUICE

1¼ CUPS (**300 ML**) GINGER JUICE
14 TBSP (**200 ML**) RICE VINEGAR

Combine the ginger juice and the rice vinegar, bring to a boil, then let cool.

34

SWEET AND SOUR RADISHES

½ CUP (**125 ML**) MUSHI SAUCE (→ SEE NO. 19)
7 TBSP (**100 ML**) RICE VINEGAR
1½ TBSP (**25 ML**) ROSE'S LEMON CORDIAL
2⅔ CUPS (**300 G**) SLICED RADISHES, CUT INTO ⅜ **IN** (**1 CM**) SLICES

In a saucepan, bring the mushi sauce, vinegar, and lemon cordial to a boil, add the radishes, and simmer for 1 minute. Strain the radishes, catching the liquid, then let both cool separately. Vacuumize the radishes and liquid together and let infuse for 24 hours.

35

SWEET AND SOUR RED ONIONS

4 CUPS (**400 G**) PEELED AND SLICED RED ONIONS
CORNISH SEA SALT
⅔ CUP (**160 ML**) RASPBERRY VINEGAR
⅓ CUP (**80 ML**) RICE VINEGAR
1 TBSP (**15 ML**) GREEN THAI PEPPERCORNS

Briefly blanch the onion slices in salted water. Put them into a vacuum bag, vacuumize and let infuse for 24 hours.

36

THAI VINAIGRETTE

7 TBSP (100 ML) VEGETABLE OIL
14 TBSP (200 ML) MUSHI SAUCE
(→ SEE NO. 19)
14 TBSP (200 ML) RICE VINEGAR
5 TBSP (80 ML) RED CHILI SAUCE
(→ SEE NO. 28)
4 TBSP (60 ML) LIME JUICE

Blend all the ingredients in a Thermomix for 3 minutes on Speed 4.

37

VANILLA BLANCMANGE

3½ TBSP (50 G) HEAVY CREAM
3½ TBSP (50 ML) MILK
A TRACE OF VANILLA SEEDS
1 EGG YOLK
1 TSP (4 G) CORNSTARCH
½ TBSP (8 G) SUGAR
30 STRIPS OF ZEST FROM UNTREATED LEMONS

In a sauté pan, bring the cream to the boil with 2 tablespoons (30 ml) milk and the vanilla seeds. Stir together the egg yolk and the cornstarch, the sugar, and the remaining milk and lemon zest, then stir into the boiling milk. Cook, stirring constantly, until the mixture starts to thicken. Take off the heat and let cool.

38

WASABI MAYONNAISE

7 TBSP (100 G) JAPANESE MAYONNAISE
⅓ CUP (40 G) GRATED FRESH WASABI
1 TBSP (15 ML) GREEN CHILI SAUCE
(→ SEE NO. 13)
1 TBSP (15 ML) TABASCO GREEN PEPPER SAUCE

Combine all the ingredients.

39

WHITE ONION CREAM

6⅔ CUPS (1 KG) PEELED AND DICED WHITE ONIONS
3⅓ CUPS (500 G) PEELED AND CHOPPED CELERY ROOT
4 TBSP (60 ML) GARLIC OIL (→ SEE NO. 9)
CORNISH SEA SALT
5 TBSP (80 ML) MILK
⅓ CUP (80 ML) CLARIFIED BUTTER
3 TBSP (40 ML) MUSHI SAUCE (→ SEE NO. 19)
1½ TBSP (20 ML) CHEF SAUCE (→ SEE NO. 2)

Put the onions, celery root, and garlic oil into a deep baking pan. Sprinkle with salt and cover with a baking sheet. Cook in the oven at 365°F (185°C) for 90 minutes. Put the cooked vegetables, milk and clarified butter into a Thermomix and blend. Season the cream with mushi sauce, chef sauce, and salt.

40

WHITE PEARL ONIONS

14 TBSP (200 ML) TARRAGON VINEGAR
14 TBSP (200 ML) JALAPEÑO MARINADE
⅔ CUP (150 G) SUGAR
6¼ CUPS (1 KG) PEELED PEARL ONIONS

In a saucepan, combine the tarragon vinegar, jalapeño marinade, and the sugar, and bring to a boil. Add the pearl onions and simmer for 10 minutes. Take off the heat and let cool. Vacuumize and let infuse for 24 hours.

41

YOUNG GINGER

2 LB 3¼ OZ (1 KG) YOUNG GINGER, UNPEELED
1¼ CUPS (300 ML) GINGER JUICE
14 TBSP (200 ML) RICE VINEGAR
⅓ CUP (100 G) AGAVE NECTAR

Cut the ginger into 1 mm slices and place them in a deep baking pan. In a saucepan, bring all the remaining ingredients to a boil. Let cool, then pour over the ginger slices and let the ginger marinate overnight.

42

YUZU MARMALADE

6 CUPS (1 KG) FINELY CHOPPED YUZU FLESH AND PEEL
14 TBSP (200 ML) YUZU JUICE
1⅔ CUP (300 G) MUSCOVADO SUGAR
2 TBSP (8 G) AGAR AGAR POWDER

In a saucepan, combine the yuzu flesh, peel, and juice with the sugar and bring to a boil. Stir in the agar agar powder and simmer for 5 minutes. Transfer the mixture to a bowl and let cool, then process in a Thermomix until smooth.

MANDARIN ORIENTAL

EXIT

비빙
KOREAN
DESSERT
CAFÉ
MASSAGE
LEVEL4
德宝
Tak Po
Hong Kong
Dim Sum
Except
Loading /
Unloading
ISUZU
YM6760K

80¢

Traditional
Ice Cream Taste
150

POP-UP NOISE: SOUL SEARCHING

CHINA TOWN
SINGAPORE

index

A

B

C

D

F

G

H

I

J

K

L

S

T

V

W

Y

Z

To-Do:
16.12:

suppliers and products

BOS FOOD

Bos Food has a selection of dry products that is unique in Europe. Its range is steadily being expanded, and you can also find some of the hardware products here. It is completely awesome, and one of the things we like best about Bos Food is the company's ability to deliver the next day.

ESPUMA FLASKS & CREAM CHARGERS BY ISI
ESPUMA THERMOS FLASKS BY ISI
EXCALIBUR DEHYDRATOR
PACOJET

BLACK WINTER TRUFFLES
WHITE ALBA TRUFFLES
ISOMALT
GLUCOSE
XANTHAN GUM, CITRAS, ELASTIC
BASIC TEXTUR
VALRHONA CHOCOLATE
CHOCOLATE CALLETS
OILS
EGG WHITE POWDER
CALPICO
IMPERIAL CAVIAR

→ WWW.BOSFOOD.DE

METRO

Metro is our newest supplier. It has a very large choice of Asian dry products, nearly as many as Asian general stores, plus the very best fish sauce by Megachef. The quality and choice of fish and crustaceans is also very good. In addition, you can find the following products here:

MINUS L DAIRY PRODUCTS
CRESS BY KOPPERT CRESS
REGIONAL GERMAN FRUIT, AND FRUIT FROM AROUND THE WORLD
ASIAN FRUIT AND VEGETABLES

→ WWW.METRO.DE

NISHIKIDÔRI MARKET

Nishikidôri Market specializes in the direct import of Japanese foods. The company is based in Paris; Europeans can comfortably order online and will receive outstanding produce that is not available from any other supplier — naturally at sky-high Japanese prices.

WASABI PASTE
KAMEBISHI SOY SAUCE
AOMORI CHILI POWDER
RICE VINEGAR
NORI SEAWEED

→ WWW.NISHIKIDORI.COM

OTTO GOURMET

The Otto brothers have supplied us with poultry, wagyu beef, game, and the rare Iberian papada for ten years. They are amazingly obsessed by quality and deliver within Germany.

→ WWW.OTTO-GOURMET.DE

VAN NAHMEN

Van Nahmen's juices are characterized by a superb balance of fruitiness and sweetness. Especially outstanding here are the rhubarb juice, the Riesling grape juice, and the quince juice.

→ WWW.VANNAHMEN.DE

WEIHE

Here restaurateurs can buy all the culinary herbs, cress by Koppert Cress, regional German and international fruit and vegetables, all the Asian fruit and vegetable products, as well as MinusL dairy products. Weihe has supplied me since 1999, making it the supplier I have worked with the longest.

→ WWW.WEIHE.DE

acknowledgments

The recipes and dishes were created by ...

TIM RAUE, CHRISTIAN SINGER,
PHILLIP BENDEL, CHRISTOPHER WECKER, DANIEL MARG,
KAI WEIGAND, ERIK SCHMITZ, JAN SEMMELHACK,
JULIAN GELDMACHER, LION SCHIRMER,
JENS HILDEBRANDT, JONAS MEROLD

With thanks to our restaurant team ...

MARIE-ANNE RAUE, ANDRÉ MACIONGA,
MELANIE REIFHOFER, BABSI GEISLER, KATHARINA BAMBACH,
CINDY KAYMLING,
SABRINA KLEWER, RAFFAEL REICHARDT, PAUL FRÖHLING,
FELIX FUCHS, DUNJA RAUER, ANNIKA KISSLING, CATHRINE HERRMANN,
THI THU HUONG TRAN, ELENA LOPEZ, HASRET ÖZDURAK,
ZOE VON PAWELSZ, EMMA HÜTT, HIJÖRDIS RÄTHER, JANA HÖNNIGE,
KEVIN TRENN

With thanks to our partners and suppliers ...

LOHBERGER KÜCHEN
ZWIESEL KRISTALLGLAS 1872
ASA SELECTION
WINTERHALTER
THERMOMIX
BER-BEK

METRO
WEIHE OBST & GEMÜSE
FRISCHEPARADIES LINDENBERG
FLEISCHEREI HÖLLERSCHMID
OTTO GOURMET
DEUTSCHE SEE
MAÎTRE PHILIPPE & FILLES
VINH-LOI
NISHIKIDÔRI MARKET
TERRA

imprint

CALLWEY
SEIT 1884

© 2017 VERLAG GEORG D.W. CALLWEY GMBH & CO. KG
STREITFELDSTRASSE 35, 81673 MUNICH, GERMANY
BUCH@CALLWEY.DE
PHONE: +49 89 436006-0

WWW.CALLWEY.DE
WWW.FACEBOOK.COM/CALLWEY
WWW.INSTAGRAM.COM/CALLWEY

ISBN 978-3-7667-2271-3
1ST EDITION 2017

GERMAN NATIONAL LIBRARY BIBLIOGRAPHICAL INFORMATION
THE GERMAN NATIONAL LIBRARY HAS LISTED THIS PUBLICATION
IN THE GERMAN NATIONAL BIBLIOGRAPHY; DETAILED BIBLIOGRAPHICAL INFORMATION
CAN BE DOWNLOADED FROM <HTTP://DNB.D-NB.DE>.

THIS BOOK IS A QUALITY PUBLICATION BY CALLWEY:
IT WAS PRINTED AND BOUND IN GERMANY BY OPTIMAL MEDIA GMBH
IN RÖBEL / MÜRITZ.

WE HOPE THAT YOU WILL ENJOY THIS BOOK:

PROJECT MANAGER: ANNE-SOPHIE ZÄHRINGER
TEXTS PART 01 AND PART 02: STEFAN ADRIAN
EDITORIAL: BOOKWISE MEDIENPRODUKTION GMBH, MUNICH
ENGLISH TRANSLATION: SYLVIA GOULDING, EMILY PLANK
COPY-EDITING AND AMERICAN EDITION: JULIE BROOKE, MIKE GOULDING
PROOFREADING: SARAH BLOXHAM, JEREMY HARWOOD
PRODUCTION: OLIVER STEHR
PHOTOGRAPHY SINGAPORE AND BERLIN: NILS HASENAU, BERLIN
FOOD PHOTOGRAPHY: JOERG LEHMANN, BERLIN
OTHER AND PERSONAL PHOTOGRAPHS: TIM RAUE
BOOK DESIGN AND ART DIRECTION: SEIDLDESIGN, STUTTGART

THE PUBLISHERS WOULD LIKE TO POINT OUT THAT PARTICULAR CARE NEEDS TO BE TA
WHEN USING LIQUID NITROGEN AS IMPROPER USE BRINGS THE RISK OF INJURY.
THE PUBLISHERS ACCEPT NO RESPONSIBILITY.